"The dreadful ignorance as to the fu   ...als of our holy religion, that almost everywhere abounds amongst the members of our established church, is chiefly owing to our neglect of preaching and putting into their hands the grand doctrines of the Reformation, contained in these *Homilies*." — **George Whitefield (1714-1770)**

"The *Homilies* are a pattern of simplicity and godly sincerity. Never was truth more plainly stated than in them. In their mode of stating divine truth, and enforcing it upon the conscience, they never have been excelled by any composition whatever. It were well if they were more regarded as a pattern for popular addresses at this day: for, in comparison of them, the great mass of public addresses, if viewed with candour and with Apostolic zeal, would be found, it is to be feared, exceedingly defective, both in energy and in scriptural instruction." — **Charles Simeon (1759-1836)**

"As an expression of the doctrine of Anglicanism in its classical period the *Homilies* of the Church of England still merit the attention not only of students but also of all who have a concern for the communication of biblical teaching. The *Homilies* should not be consigned to the unremembered past." — **Philip Edgcumbe Hughes (1915-1990), Secretary of Church Society and Editor of *Churchman***

"Lee Gatiss has done us all an immense favour and blessing. Honestly how many of us can say that we know and love the Homilies? But here we have up to date language and inspirational content. In short, I commend this book to you as being challenging, educational, readable, relevant, and necessary for all serious Anglicans throughout the world."—**Bishop Henry Scriven, General Secretary of the Evangelical Fellowship of the Anglican Communion**

"In a famous essay 'On the reading of old books,' C. S. Lewis made the point that the only way in which we can avoid being trapped by the thinking of the present is to read books from the past. In his words, 'The only palliative is to keep the clean sea breeze of the centuries blowing through our minds, and this can be done only by reading old books.'

Among the old books that Anglicans in particular ought to be reading are the First and Second Books of *Homilies* produced by the Church of England in the sixteenth century. As Article XXXV of the Thirty Nine Articles tell us, these two collections of Homilies, or sermons, 'contain a godly and wholesome doctrine' and they provide a deeply challenging alternative to the theology which prevails in the Church of England today.

Unfortunately, readers unacquainted with sixteenth-century English can find the *Homilies* hard to understand, not because of what they say, but simply because of the now archaic way in which they say it. Fortunately, Lee Gatiss has addressed this situation by producing an excellent new edition of the *Homilies* which retains the bulk of the original wording, but updates those archaic words and phrases that are most likely to confuse or mislead the average reader today. He also provides a helpful introduction, a foreword written by the great eighteenth-century Evangelical George Whitefield, and notes all the biblical references in the *Homilies* plus the references to the Apocrypha and the writings of the Church Fathers.

This is an enormously helpful resource which should be read by all those in training for ordained or lay Anglican ministry and by all other Anglicans who want to learn from the wisdom of our Anglican forebears about how to think rightly about the theological and ethical issues we face today."—**Martin Davie, Theological Consultant to the Church of England Evangelical Council**

THE FIRST BOOK OF

HOMILIES

The Church of England's
Official Sermons in Modern English

EDITED & INTRODUCED BY
Lee Gatiss

FOREWORD BY
George Whitefield

LOST C●IN

Church
Society

EQUIPPING GOD'S
PEOPLE TO LIVE
GOD'S WORD

The First Book of Homilies Edited by Lee Gatiss

© Church Society/Lost Coin Books, 2021.

Published for Church Society by Lost Coin Books, London.
email: lostcoinbooks@gmail.com
web: www.lostcoinbooks.com   LOST C●IN

Church Society
www.churchsociety.org
admin@churchsociety.org

Church Society, Ground Floor, Centre Block
Hille Business Estate, 132 St Albans Road
Watford WD24 4AE, UK
Tel +44 (0)1923 255410

ISBN 978-1-7399376-0-7

Contents

ABBREVIATIONS

ANF *Ante-Nicene Fathers*
(edited by Alexander Roberts and James Donaldson; New York, 1885)

ESV *English Standard Version*

KJV *King James Version* (1611)

LCL *The Loeb Classical Library*
(London: William Heineman, various dates)

NETS *A New English Translation of the Septuagint*
(edited by Albert Pietersma and Benjamin G. Wright; Oxford: Oxford University Press, 2014)

NIV *New International Version*

NPNF *The Nicene and Post-Nicene Fathers*
(edited by Philip Schaff; New York, 1886)

NPNF2 *The Nicene and Post-Nicene Fathers: Second Series*
(edited by Philip Schaff and Henry Wace; New York, 1890)

NRSV *New Revised Standard Version*

PG Jacques-Paul Migne (ed.), *Patrologiae Cursus Completus: Patrologia Graeca* 161 volumes (1857-1866)

PL Jacques-Paul Migne (ed.), *Patrologiae Cursus Completus: Patrologia Latina* 217 volumes (1841-1855)

INTRODUCTION

A few years ago I posted some daily readings from the official Anglican Homilies on the Church Society blog during Lent. I updated the English as I went, for the sake of a modern audience. This created some renewed interest in these wonderful old sermons, and a demand for a full, book-length publication. As the *Homilies* have always been an important part of the official formularies, which define and expound the inheritance of faith which Anglicans are to proclaim afresh in each generation, that seemed a worthy and worthwhile thing to do. It is especially important in an age where Anglicanism worldwide seems to be in the midst of an identity crisis. I have spoken elsewhere of an Anglican *midlife crisis*; and what is needed at such a time is not to give in to doubt, division, or despair, but to return to the stabilising roots from which Anglicanism has drawn its vital spark, its vivacity, and its vigour.[1] We face again what King Edward VI calls in his original preface to the *Homilies*, the great decay of Christian religion and the utter destruction of innumerable souls through hypocrisy and harmful doctrine. This is what makes returning to the *Homilies* such an invigorating and useful thing to do today.

The publication of these sermons in 1547 by Archbishop Cranmer was originally intended to play a part in reforming and renewing the Church of England in biblical faith. As Ashley Null has written, "the *Book of Homilies* was designed to be a manifesto of the regime's theological agenda and the means of its revolutionary implementation."[2] The *Homilies* were designed to intro-

---

1   Lee Gatiss, *The True Profession of the Gospel: Augustus Toplady and Reclaiming our Reformed Foundations* (London: Latimer Trust, 2010), 3-7.

2   Ashley Null, "Official Tudor Homilies" in Peter McCulloch, Hugh Adlington, and Emma Rhatigan (eds.), *The Oxford Handbook of the Early Modern Sermon*

duce a biblically-starved people to doctrinally-healthy teaching in their own language, such as they had never experienced before in a regular and systematic way. Just as the majestic language of the later *Book of Common Prayer* "passionately pleaded with people to engage their hearts in serving a merciful God, who sent his Son to save wretched sinners by faith alone,"[3] so too did the *Homilies*. They were also meant to function as a doctrinal formulary, a standard of teaching. Word-for-word agreement with them was not demanded, as if they were in themselves infallible. Clergy were told, however, that they "should not at any time or place preach, or set forth unto the people, any doctrine contrary or repugnant to the effect and intent contained or set forth in the King's highness' homilies."[4] As Carl Trueman rightly says,

"Thus, the production of homilies was in part a response to what we might call the pastoral crisis precipitated by the Reformation. The parish priest may well have been an ignorant fellow who could not even name the four Gospel writers, let alone list the Old Testament prophetic books in order, but if he was basically literate then he could feed his people by reading a set homily at each service. The homilies were thus one means by which the Reformation Anglican Church sought to fulfill Paul's mandate of holding fast to a form of sound words and passing on the faith from place to place and generation to generation."[5]

It is thought that the weekly reading of the set *Homilies* in church would eventually become unnecessary, however, when a regular supply of trustworthy preachers could be trained and appointed to churches. Reading the *Homilies* would be an excellent temporary measure, until the supply of competent preachers could meet the

---

(Oxford: Oxford University Press, 2011), 348.

3   Lee Gatiss, *Light After Darkness: How the Reformers Regained, Retold, and Relied On the Gospel of Grace* (Fearn, Ross-shire: Christian Focus, 2019), 123.

4   Null, "Official Tudor Homilies", 352 quoting from the Injunctions issued the same day as the *Homilies*.

5   Carl R Trueman, *The Creedal Imperative* (Wheaton, IL.: Crossway, 2012), 112.

demand created by the nation's new allegiance to the Reformation. Fewer than half the London clergy were licensed to preach their own sermons in 1560, but there was a steady rise in university-educated ministers, so that by 1601, the proportion had doubled to 88%.[6] The Archbishop of Canterbury, Edmund Grindal (1519-1583) fell out with Queen Elizabeth I during this period, since she considered the *Homilies* more a permanent solution than a short-term necessity, whereas Grindal was keen to see freshly-composed and locally-applied preaching in every pulpit, not simply set sermons.[7] Often, it was possible to have both, with the *Homilies* later being used on Sunday evenings, for example, when the Vicar had preached his own sermon in the morning. But the original Reformers, as Philip Edgcumbe Hughes says,

> "were unwilling to envisage the Homilies as a permanent alternative to preaching, and accordingly they looked and laboured for the time when the supply of good preachers would be so plentiful that the reading of homilies at public worship would become a thing of the past. The second-best was to be superseded by the best. But, again, it was not the teaching of the Homilies but the method that would become outmoded."[8]

THE DOCTRINE OF THE HOMILIES

So what is the teaching of the *Homilies*? When presenting one's theology, there are two common starting points. We may begin with God, or with our means of knowing him. The *Thirty-nine Articles* begin with God the Trinity, whereas the *Homilies* adopt

---

6   Paul Seaver, *The Puritan Lectureships: The Politics of Religious Dissent 1560-1662* (Stanford: Stanford University Press, 1970), 130. See Lee Gatiss, "To Satisfy People's Hunger for the Word: St Antholin's as the Prototype Puritan Lectureship" in Gatiss (ed.), *Pilgrims, Warriors, and Servants: Puritan Wisdom for Today's Church* (London: Latimer Trust, 2010), 19.

7   See "The Ordinary Instrument of Salvation: Edmund Grindal on Preaching" in Lee Gatiss, *Cornerstones of Salvation: Foundations and Debates in the Reformed Tradition* (Welwyn: Evangelical Press, 2017), 93-115.

8   Philip Edgcumbe Hughes, "Preaching, Homilies, and Prophesyings in Sixteenth Century England" in *The Churchman* 89.1 (1975), 21.

the alternative approach and start with the doctrine of scripture (as confessions such as the Westminster Confession of Faith also do). There is no contradiction of substance here of course, just a difference of purpose and method. The *Thirty-nine Articles* begin with the classical doctrine of God which the Protestant Church of England shared with Rome. They then build on this to show how Reformed doctrine is a harmonious development from the universal or catholic doctrine of the early and medieval church. The *Homilies*, on the other hand, begin by showing people that the way to know God and what he wants from us is not to look to Rome for infallible guidance, but to go back to the scriptures, "the food of the soul." This is presented as a catholic doctrine (small 'c'), with big names from the early church such as Chrysostom and Augustine brought in to convince us of its ancient credentials. It is not novel in Christian history to turn to the Bible, despite the objections of those who claim it is too difficult for ordinary churchgoers to understand. So as the first Homily says, "What excuse shall we therefore make at the last day before Christ, if we delight to read or hear human fantasies and inventions more than his most holy gospel, and will find no time to do that which chiefly above all things we should do?"

After this, the *Homilies* show us how we are more sinful and lost than we could ever imagine but also more loved by a merciful God than we could ever dream. The Homily on "the misery of all mankind" which outlines the doctrine of the Fall and sin, was originally written by John Harpsfield (1516–1578) of New College, Oxford. Sadly, Harpsfield himself eventually persecuted leading Reformers because of his view of the Pope's authority. His Homily contains several quotations from the apocryphal books, which were rejected as part of scripture by Protestants. As the *Thirty-nine Articles* say, these extra books are not part of holy scripture as such, yet may be read "for example of life and instruction of manners", although the church "does not apply them to establish any doctrine" (Article 6). On the subject of sin, the Apocrypha are in entire agreement with the scriptures which Harpsfield also quotes from. In the careful way that Cranmer has arranged the order of the *Homilies*, the common doctrine of original sin presented here becomes the necessary backdrop for understanding the Protestant doctrine of salvation in Cranmer's next Homily.

According to the *Thirty-nine Articles*, the Homily of Salvation or Homily of Justification outlines "a most wholesome doctrine", that "we are justified by Faith only". The justice and mercy of God are the only answer to the human predicament created by our original and actual sin. Only Christ can save us, says Cranmer, and he has: "by shedding his most precious blood, he made a sacrifice and satisfaction, or (as we might say) he made amends to his Father for our sins, to satisfy the wrath and indignation he had against us for them." Those who turn to God are "washed by this sacrifice from their sins, in such a way that there remains no spot of sin that shall be imputed to their damnation." All this is not through our own good works or because we earn or deserve it, but only by grace and only through faith. This Homily goes out of its way to demonstrate how its teaching of "justification by faith alone" is not a new invention, but the loud and clear testimony of the early and medieval church. There are more footnotes in this Homily than any other, because Cranmer quotes here from so many other scholars and sources to convince us of the catholicity or universality of this often misunderstood doctrine.

The following homilies outline the life of faith, hope, and love which a justified sinner is delighted to lead. "The thrust of the Homilies," as Philip Edgcumbe Hughes wrote, "is ethical as well as doctrinal; for the Reformers perceived, in line with the plain teaching of the apostles themselves, that right faith must go hand in hand with right conduct."[9] Cranmer can even include a homily originally penned by Bishop Bonner (1500-1569), another Roman Catholic opponent of Protestants, on the subject of Christian love. But again, placed in the context of his own sermons on scrip-

---

9   Hughes, "Preaching, Homilies, and Prophesying", 8.

ture and salvation, Cranmer makes Bonner speak good Protestant sense. As Ashley Null puts it, "the handiwork of the staunchly traditionalist Bonner now functioned as the fullest expression of the life to be lived by those assured of their salvation by grace alone though faith alone."[10]

The *Homilies* move from scripture to sin, and then from salvation to sanctification, but often in a surprising way. After the Homily on Love, there is a sermon on making and breaking oaths, which may seem to us to be an unusual place to go next (when did you last hear a sermon on this subject?). In the context of the recent Wars of the Roses, and the threat of societal breakdown all over Europe at that time, it may not however have been so remarkable.[11] The "swearing" spoken of in this homily is not so much about profanities or coarse and rude words, as swearing oaths in a legal or commercial setting. The Homily on obedience to authorities was also extremely important to Tudor monarchs keen to enforce their will in every part of the kingdom. It remains relevant for Christians in a disobedient, cynical, and often unruly world, where our culture's attitude to established authorities is not always very respectful.

The two homilies on falling away from God, and the fear of death are more pastoral and spiritual in focus. Life is always precarious and uncertain, as the recent global pandemic has surely reminded the twenty-first century, but in the sixteenth century, anxiety about death could be an ever-present reality. As Calvin so memorably put it:

---

10   Null, "Official Tudor Homilies", 357. In his *Thomas Cranmer's Doctrine of Repentance: Renewing the Power to Love* (Oxford: Oxford University Press, 2000), 215-217, Null agrees with the work of R. C. Jenkins that Cranmer even borrowed from the work of Luther's great opponent, Cardinal Cajetan to make some of his points in the Homily on Justification, thus showing that "in his homilies as in his liturgical work, Cranmer drew upon a variety of sources to find the best linguistic expression of the doctrine he wished to promote" (page 220).

11   Indeed, Calvin preached against perjury in 1554 as if it was also a common problem in Geneva around the same time. See John Calvin, *Sermons on First Timothy* (trans. Robert White; Edinburgh: Banner of Truth, 2018), 42-43.

"Innumerable are the evils that beset human life; innumerable too, the deaths that threaten it… Now, wherever you turn, all things around you not only are hardly to be trusted but almost openly menace, and seem to threaten immediate death. Embark upon a ship, you are one step away from death. Mount a horse, if one foot slips, your life is imperiled. Go through the city streets, you are subject to as many dangers as there are tiles on the roofs… Your house, continually in danger of fire, threatens in the daytime to impoverish you, at night even to collapse upon you. Your field, since it is exposed to hail, frost, drought, and other calamities, threatens you with barrenness, and hence, famine. I pass over poisonings, ambushes, robberies, open violence, which in part besiege us at home, in part dog us abroad. Amid these tribulations must not man be most miserable, since, but half alive in life, he weakly draws his anxious and languid breath, as if he had a sword perpetually hanging over his neck?"[12]

Like Calvin, the *Homilies*, however, urge us not to fear death but to trust in God's providence and promises. For believers know, says the Homily, that "death shall be to them no death at all, but truly a deliverance from death, and from all the pains, cares, and sorrows, miseries, and wretchedness of this world. It will truly be an entrance into rest, and a beginning of everlasting joy."

Thomas Becon (1511-1567), a Reformer from Norwich, then gives us a classic statement of Anglican sexual ethics, in the Homily on adultery and sexual sin. Like all the *Homilies*, this one does not simply seek to inform us (as much preaching does today), and it certainly does not seek merely to entertain; it's purpose is to turn our stomachs, to provoke an emotional reaction in us so that "your stomachs may be moved to rise against it, and to detest and abhor that sin which is so much to be hated." Sexual sin was "so abundantly common and has grown to such a height that among many it is counted no sin at all," Becon preached. He carefully worked through the teaching of Jesus and his apostles on the sub-

---

12 John Calvin, *Institutes of the Christian Religion* (edited by J. T. McNeill and translated by F. L. Battles; Louisville, KY: Westminster John Knox Press, 2011), 1:223-225 (1.17.10-11).

ject, to show how much God is opposed to sex outside of marriage between a man and a woman, according to the scriptures. He lamented the disease, illegitimacy, economic cost, and contention that arose because of sexual sin. He asked, with some sadness, "How much is God's word regarded with contempt and distorted by sexual sin and those who are sexually immoral?" It is disappointing that even though the *Homilies* do get a mention in the Church of England's recent book on sexuality, *Living in Love and Faith*, there is not even a passing glance at this particular homily, which could surely make a valuable contribution to contemporary debates over sexuality.[13]

Given that there is so much argument and strife over that subject in the church today, it is fitting that the final homily in this book is the *Homily against Contention and Brawling*. This laments the disunity of the church and the impatient pride of Christians. "Let us so read the scripture that by reading it we may be made better livers, rather than more contentious disputers," it says. We are urged not to revile when we are reviled, or to argue with the argumentative, for "a special remedy against malicious tongues is to arm ourselves with patience, meekness, and silence; lest with multiplying words with the enemy, we are made as evil as them." This is certainly a homily for the social media age. As it says, using an example from ancient Greece, "Pericles was provoked to anger by many insulting words, but answered not a word. But we, stirred by one little word—what tragedies do we claim! How do we fume, rage, stamp and stare like mad men! Many people make a great matter out of every trifle, and with the spark of a little word will kindle a great fire, taking everything in the worst possible way."

It is striking that despite the stress of the *Homilies* on scripture as the source of our theology, they do often bring in the words of

---

13   *Living in Love and Faith: Christian Teaching and Learning about Identity, Sexuality, Relationships and Marriage* (London: Church House Publishing, 2020). There are very brief mentions of the Homily on Scripture and (from the *Second Book of Homilies*) the Homily on the State of Matrimony.

other ancient preachers and theologians too (as can be seen here in the footnotes and Glossary). This is not to put the examples of the ancient Greeks or the words of the early church fathers on a par with scripture. By no means. As the Italian Reformer, Peter Martyr Vermigli (1499-1562) said,

> "For even if all the Fathers shall consent among themselves, yet we will not do this injury to the Holy Spirit, that we should rather give credit to them than to the word of God. Indeed, the Fathers themselves would never want themselves to be so believed, as they have sufficiently testified in their writings that they will not have that honour to be given to them, but to the holy scriptures alone. So those who appeal from the scriptures to the Fathers, appeal to the Fathers against the Fathers."[14]

The use of so many voices from church history demonstrates that Reformed teaching is a restoration of an ancient Christian tradition—shared by Ambrose, Anselm, Augustine, Basil, Bernard, Chomatius, Chrysostom, Cyprian, Didymus, Fulgentius, Gregory, Hilary, Jerome, Martin of Tours, Oecumenius, Origen, Photius, Prosper, and Theophylact. It also shows that the Protestant Church of England is part of a global and diverse civilisation that had been represented in Italy, Algeria, Turkey, France, Tunisia, Egypt, Croatia, North Macedonia, and elsewhere. It has since, of course, spread even further around the world. Reformation Anglicanism is not afraid to learn from a wide range of people, who are all committed to the "one, holy, catholic, and apostolic faith" (as the Nicene Creed puts it). It is also not afraid to apply that faith in an inclusive way, "to all kinds of people, all degrees and all ages" (as Homily 11 puts it).

---

14 Peter Martyr Vermigli, *The Common Places of the Most Famous and Renowned Divine Doctor Peter Martyr* (London: Henry Denham and Henry Middleton, 1583), 4:48-9 (I have updated the language). Vermigli was born in Florence, Italy but moved to England in 1547 to become Regius Professor of Divinity at Oxford and a key influence on Cranmer and the English Reformation.

EVANGELICAL USE OF THE HOMILIES

English Reformers such as Bishop Nicholas Ridley (1500-1555) were delighted by the "holy and wholesome" *Homilies,* and enjoined the clergy to read them to their congregations.[15] Protestants elsewhere in Europe were also pleased to read the *Homilies.* John Strype (1643-1737) records that the First Book of Homilies "caused great rejoicing" when it came to Strasbourg and the community of Protestants there in 1547. The Reformer Martin Bucer (1491-1551) wrote a "gratulatory epistle" to the Church of England for such well-explained teaching, which he was sure would have a positive effect.[16]

During the Revival of the eighteenth century, Anglican Evangelicals were keen to identify their own doctrines with those contained in the Anglican formularies, not least the *Homilies.* The Anglican methodist preacher, John Fletcher of Madeley (1729-1785) noted in a letter that he preached one of the *Homilies* on a Sunday evening, and he often pointed to them to defend his own teaching.[17] William Grimshaw of Haworth (1708-1763) had a similar respect for them, and considered it his duty to read them annually, convinced that if others also did so, they too would become zealous evangelicals.[18] Augustus Toplady (1740-1778) often pointed to the *Homilies* to demonstrate what he called the doctrinal Calvinism of the Church of England: "These homilies are still a part of our ecclesiastical establishment," he asserted, "Let any man but read them; and then doubt if he can, whether the composers were not Calvinists."[19] As we can see from his preface to the *Homilies*

---

15 See *The Works of Nicholas Ridley* (ed. Henry Christmas; Cambridge: Cambridge University Press, 1841), 320, 400

16 John Strype, *Ecclesiastical Memorials: Relating Chiefly to Religion, and the Reformation of It. Volume 2, Part 1* (Oxford: Clarendon Press, 1822), 49-51.

17 See *The Works of the Rev. John Fletcher* (London: John Mason, 1859), 1:72, 76; 2:218, 489, 512, 514 (1833).

18 See J. C. Ryle, *Christian Leaders of the Last Century* (London: T. Nelson and Sons, 1869), 114, 129-130.

19 See Augustus Montague Toplady, *The Historic Proof of the Doctrinal Calvinism of*

below, and elsewhere in his works, the great Anglican evangelist George Whitefield (1714-1770) was also a fan of the *Homilies*, even insisting that they be read by the children in his orphanage in Georgia every year.[20]

In 1812, the Prayer Book and Homily Society was formed, supported primarily by evangelicals, to publish Prayer Books and Homilies in English, as well as translating the former into many other languages. Anglican evangelicals remained convinced of the usefulness of these sixteenth-century sermons, despite being keen to preach in their own words from the pulpit. As Charles Simeon of Cambridge (1759-1836) said,

> "The Homilies are a pattern of simplicity and godly sincerity. Never was truth more plainly stated than in them. The language in which they are written is indeed antiquated; in consequence of which, the use of them has been discontinued: but, in their mode of stating divine truth, and enforcing it upon the conscience, they never have been excelled by any composition whatever. It were well if they were more regarded as a pattern for popular addresses at this day: for, in comparison of them, the great mass of public addresses, if viewed with candour and with Apostolic zeal, would be found, it is to be feared, exceedingly defective, both in energy and in scriptural instruction."[21]

In the twentieth century, my predecessor at Church Society (and editor of *Churchman*), Philip Edgcumbe Hughes (1915-1990), wrote that: "As an expression of the doctrine of Anglicanism in its classical period the Homilies of the Church of England still merit the attention not only of students but also of all who have a concern for the communication of biblical teaching. The Homilies

---

the *Church of England* (London, 1774), 1:287-288 (§13).

20 See Lee Gatiss, "George Whitefield—The Anglican Evangelist" in Benjamin Dean and Adriaan Neele (eds.), *The Genius of George Whitefield: Reflections on his Ministry from 21st Century Africa* (London: Latimer Trust, 2015), 1-3.

21 Charles Simeon *Horae Homileticae: Volume 12. Mark-Luke* (London: Holdsworth and Ball, 1832), 436–437.

should not be consigned to the unremembered past."[22] For this reason, twentieth-century evangelical leaders such as Jim Packer (1926-2020) and John Stott (1921-2011) would often quote from the *Homilies* in their own books, to keep alive the remembrance of them and their eloquent expression of the central truths of the faith.[23] As Anglican Evangelicals, they and other leaders were always keen to stress that Anglicanism is not a brand of liberal Catholicism, as some would have it be. As Gerald Bray puts it, "Not the least of GAFCON's merits is the way in which it has called us back to the study of Anglicanism's true theological foundations in the Thirty-nine Articles of Religion, the *Homilies* and the Book of Common Prayer."[24] Therefore, as we face the ecclesiastical crises and controversies of our own day, we must remember what Mark Thompson so stirringly says:

> "The *Articles*, *The Book of Common Prayer* (especially in its 1552 form), and *The Book of Homilies*, are full of evangelical theology. It is worth reminding ourselves of these things in the midst of our present struggle. We can be worn down and actually start believing the rhetoric that is thrown at us. Let them say we are an aberrant minority which has recently emerged and is trying to take over what has always been a more catholic and liberal institution. An honest evaluation of the facts shows that is far from the case. The Church of England was born out of that struggle for the truth which we call the Reformation. Its founders were among the first Reformation martyrs in this country. What is more, the Reformers' appeal to the Fathers was on the basis that we are the true Catholics!"[25]

---

22 Hughes, "Preaching, Homilies, and Prophesyings", 21.

23 E.g. J. I. Packer, *God Has Spoken: Revelation and the Bible* (London: Hodder & Stoughton, 1993), 42-43 (on scripture), and John Stott, *Evangelical Truth: A Personal Plea for Unity* (Leicester: IVP, 1999), 92 (on the cross).

24 Gerald Bray, "Editorial: Crime and Punishment" in *Churchman* 122.4 (2008), 295.

25 Mark D. Thompson, "Being Clearly and Positively Evangelical" in *Churchman* 111.2 (1997), 168.

THIS EDITION OF THE HOMILIES

This is not a critical edition of an ancient text for academic purposes. The majority of scholars who need it can have access to the original sixteenth-century text through Early English Books Online or a research library if close study is necessary. I have used such original documents in compiling this edition,[26] but not sought to replicate them in every tiny detail. Rather, this is a lightly edited version of the original 1547 text in modern English, with a few subsequent clarifications and divisions from later authorised editions.[27] I have tried to retain as far as possible the literary beauty and force of the original, for the sake of those who need and want to have access to the edifying doctrine of this book.

I have inserted biblical references into the text, including those which were originally noted in the margins of the 1547 edition. Where the *Homilies* cite or quote from other authors, I have noted the source whenever I could by reasonable effort determine it, should people want to chase those up in standard editions of the original Latin and Greek, as well as in recent English translations. References to the Apocrypha are treated as secondary sources, rather than noted as biblical references, and so appear in the footnotes. I have updated the spelling and punctuation, and felt free to change colons and semi-colons if I felt there was a hindrance to clarity for the modern reader. Paragraph breaks have sometimes been added to give the reader a chance to breathe. The early editions often differed in such details anyway.

I have modernised various archaic, obscure, or obsolete words,

---

26 Specifically, *Certayne Sermons, or homelies, appoynted by the kynges Maiestie, to be declared and redde, by all persones, Vicars, or Curates, every Sondaye in their churches, where they have Cure* (1547) which is in the British Museum.

27 I have consulted e.g. John Griffiths (ed.), *The Two Books of Homilies Appointed to be Read in Churches* (Oxford: Oxford University Press, 1859), as well as Ronald B. Bond, *Certain Sermons or Homilies (1547) and A Homily against Disobedience and Wilful Rebellion (1570): A Critical Edition* (London: University of Toronto Press, 1987), and Gerald Bray (ed.), *The Books of Homilies: A Critical Edition* (Cambridge: James Clarke and Co, 2015). I have re-checked every citation I picked up from them, and made several corrections as necessary.

e.g. "heretofore", "forasmuch", and "minished". This edition speaks of the *cancellation* of debts or sins, rather than of *remission*, and of *unbelievers* rather than *heathens*. It often speaks of us as *pitiable* rather than *miserable*, where that might create confusion about whether it means our mental unhappiness or our sinful state. Where necessary, I have made the sermons refer to people and mankind, or our ways, *human* ways rather than speaking of man and men exclusively, unless male persons are specifically in view. This is so that the intent of the original authors is made undistractingly clearer to twenty-first century readers. In any case, the *Homilies* themselves originally spoke often of "persons" in some places, not simply generic "men", and sometimes "his" and "our" were interchanged in different early modern editions.[28]

Where a word in the *Homilies* is still used today but has changed its meaning, I have substituted a modern equivalent. For example, the homily against contention and brawling (Homily 12) speaks about arguments going "from hot words to further inconvenience"—yet the meaning is hardly that the argument is not convenient at that time or place (which seems rather a mild point), but that it descends from angry words to something worse: from hot words to further *impropriety* (or improper behaviour). Elsewhere in the *Homilies*, the word "inconvenient" was used more in the sense of "not fitting" or "inappropriate", and so I have used those more suitable equivalents to convey the meaning.

I have also updated all the archaic *-eth* verb endings and clarified some sentence structures. I know that some will lament the loss of archaic style and old vocabulary, and this pleaseth not the purists, but it makes the text far easier for a modern reader to follow. It is clear from studying the different sixteenth- and seventeenth-century editions of the *Homilies* that there were small changes made over this period to vocabulary and expressions in the published texts. Clarifications were added or words were changed,

---

28 See, for example, Griffiths, *The Two Books of Homilies*, 79 and Bray, *The Books of Homilies*, 64.

as the English language developed and efforts were made to make these sermons more intelligible to their audiences.[29] I am merely continuing that pre-existing development here. After all, Article 35 says that the Homilies are meant to be "understanded of by the people" (*sic*), not puzzled over and deciphered.

I have split each Homily into two or three parts, as was first done (rather oddly in some places) in 1549. Two years of experience convinced many users of the first edition that shorter sermons might have greater effect, though some, such as the Reformer Martin Bucer, were not impressed by this pandering tactic. As one editor says, the original *Homilies* "appear to have made in this instance too little allowance for the ignorance of the very rudiments of Christian truth in which the uneducated classes in the country had been kept so long, and the indifference, not to say disrelish, to it thereby engendered."[30] In my experience, each "part" takes around 10-15 minutes to preach which may, even now, be considered too long a sermon for some, but all should aspire to a greater appetite for the preached word of God.[31] I have added subheadings and given each "part" its own title, to aid the reader in appreciating the basic thrust of each section and the flow of the argument.

I also include below an edited version of the foreword to the *Homilies* written by the great eighteenth-century evangelist George Whitefield. He planned in his day to produce a cheap edition of the *Homilies*, in order to remedy the great ignorance of Church of England ministers and congregations about the "grand doctrines of the Reformation."[32] This would also demonstrate, in

---

29 Even between the first and second editions of 1547 there were small changes to "mend" the English and correct or refine the style. Strype, *Ecclesiastical Memorials. Volume 2, Part 1*, 49.

30 Griffiths, *The Two Books of Homilies*, xi.

31 I preached through the *Homilies* myself in a modernised version on the Church Society website and YouTube channel each weekday in Lent 2021.

32 Whitefield's edition was also to contain a prayer and a suggested hymn to sing after each homily, because true Reformation theology leads inexorably to heartfelt prayer and praise. See *The Works of the Reverend George Whitefield: Volume IV* (London, 1771), pages 441-454. Cf pages 334-335 for part of his letter to Revd

times of confusion, the loyalty of Reformed Evangelical Anglicans to the doctrinal foundations of Anglicanism. That has also been my goal here. We may not necessarily agree with Whitefield that these *Homilies* should still be read out in church services today. We might prefer to have the same doctrine delivered to us in freshly-written, specially-composed sermons from well-trained contemporary preachers who know their own congregations well. Whitefield himself did exemplify that and encouraged others in it. Where such solid food cannot be easily obtained, however, we could do worse than serve up the sort of rich and edifying diet which these *Homilies* represent. They do, after all, bear witness to Christian truth as we in the Church of England have received it. Better half a loaf of bread than no bread at all, as Archbishop Grindal once said; and certainly better an edifying old Homily than mouldy, indigestible half-baked nonsense.

Thanks are due to my son and editorial assistant, Joshua Gatiss, for carefully reading through the text and suggesting numerous improvements for readability. I also wish to thank the diligent David Meager for his help in proof reading and compiling the scripture index—another way in which he has faithfully served Church Society in his 20 years of service with us.

LEE GATISS
Cambridge
July, 2021

Dr Durell on the same subject (from April 1768).

FOREWORD

The word *homily* signifies a sermon. Consequently "the Book of Homilies", implies a book of sermons. Particularly that book which was composed by those great reformers—Cranmer, Ridley, Latimer, Hooper, and others—in the beginning of the reign of that Josiah of his age, Edward VI. It was again republished, after the short interval of bloody Mary's government, in the reign of Queen Elizabeth I, and continued interwoven with our ecclesiastical constitution, under her immediate successor King James I. Even to this very day, the thirty-fifth Article of our church says thus:

> "The second book of Homilies, the several titles whereof we have joined under this Article, doth contain a godly and wholesome doctrine, and necessary for these times; as doth the former Book of Homilies, which were set forth in the time of Edward VI; and therefore we judge them to be read in churches by the ministers, diligently and distinctly, that they may be understanded of by the people."

Such are the express words of our 35th Article; and yet, though we subscribe this Article, which enjoins these *Homilies* to be read in our churches by the ministers, diligently and distinctly, this is so far from being our practice, that almost for time immemorial, at least in our days, they are seldom if ever read at all. What reason can be assigned for such neglect, I will not take upon myself to determine. Surely it cannot be that our clergy look upon this book as containing *un*-godly or *un*-wholesome doctrine—for why then do they subscribe to the diligent and frequent reading of it? Neither can it be supposed that they so much as imagine that this godly and wholesome doctrine is less necessary for the present age, than for that in which it was first published.

But however it is, if we act confidently, the subscribers to our Articles seem not to be left at their liberty to use or disuse them; they being judged to be read, as much now as formerly, "in churches by the ministers, diligently and distinctly." For if I may be suffered to give my opinion, the dreadful ignorance as to the fundamentals of our holy religion, that almost everywhere abounds amongst the members of our established church, is chiefly owing to our neglect of preaching and putting into their hands the grand doctrines of the Reformation, contained in these *Homilies* and our other doctrinal articles. And hence undoubtedly it is, that they become such an easy prey to those who lie in wait to deceive.

For these reasons, in order to contribute my small coin (Luke 21:2) towards putting a stop to the growth of this common and almost epidemical evil, I have selected a few of the most essential *Homilies*, with a suitable collect and a hymn to each, at a very small price, on purpose for the instruction and edification of the poorer sort.

The Church of Scotland, called our sister church, has set us an example in this. I could wish, that in this particular we would endeavour to copy it. Her confessions of faith, and directory, are printed so frequently and so cheap, that they are almost in every hand. They are so constantly explained and insisted upon by ministers in their parish visits that their doctrine is extremely well known. Would to God the same could be said of members of the Church of England, either at home or abroad! The darkness, the gross and thick darkness of those at home, is so notorious, that it is everywhere seen, felt, and complained of, by those that have eyes to see and ears to hear.

What a pity is it therefore, that this *Book of Homilies* is not judged proper, and insisted on to be read in churches, by ministers diligently and distinctly, that they may be understood by the people now, as well as at the first dawnings of the Reformation.

And what a further pity is it, that among the various books recommended and given away by the worthy societies for promoting Christian knowledge, and propagating the gospel in foreign parts, the *Book of Homilies*, containing such "godly and wholesome doctrine diligently and distinctly to be read", should never find a place in their catalogue; though both these societies have been established so long as soon after the glorious and happy revolution.[1]

If our societies at home, or missionaries abroad, should urge in excuse for their not reading or distributing this book of *Homilies*, that its language and diction is too antique and obsolete; I humbly apprehend, they might with equal propriety make the same objection against the use of, and distribution of the *Book of Common Prayer*. For both were compiled by the same great luminaries of our Church, and that too in the very same important era of the Reformation. Both contain the same godly and wholesome doctrine, and both are equally adapted to instruct the ignorant, and at the same time to raise and elevate the devout and simple heart. And therefore since the one is constantly to be read from the lectern, why should not the other be diligently and distinctly read and enforced from the pulpit?[2]

Would to God that this was our universal practice: for then our daily or weekly worshippers and hearers, would not only be taught the first principles and doctrines of Christ, in a language suitable to their capacities; but—which alas! alas! has been too too long the case of the lectern and pulpit—the lectern and pulpit would not frequently and so wretchedly oppose and contradict each other. Heterodoxy and mere worldly morality would then no longer be our famous declamatory topics. Those who, after the strictest and most impartial examination, must be considered to adhere most

---

1   Whitefield refers to the SPCK (1698) and SPGFP (1701), both founded within a few years of the Glorious Revolution when William and Mary came to the throne in 1688.

2   In the original, Whitefield contrasts the pulpit with "the desk", meaning not the place of study but the place from which the *Book of Common Prayer* was read and prayed by the minister in church.

steadily to the *Homilies*, Articles, and Liturgy of the Church of England would not be deemed "enthusiasts" and cast out as madmen, troublers of Israel, setters forth of strange doctrines, and turners of the world and church upside down. At the same time, they must also endeavour to adorn her godly and wholesome doctrines contained in these formularies (as being in their judgments the doctrines of their Lord and Saviour Jesus Christ) with an appropriate lifestyle.

If this is to be vile, God grant they may be more vile! If this is enthusiasm, God grant it a universal flow! For the consequence I know will be, that not only our own, but every Protestant Reformed church, would then not only be a common barrier against popery and profaneness, but would shine as bright as the sun, be as fair as the moon, and terrible like an army with banners (Song of Songs 6:10).

That this may be our happy case, is the hearty prayer, Christian reader, of your servant,

GEORGE WHITEFIELD

THE PREFACE

The King's most excellent Majesty has caused this book of *Homilies* to be made and set forth by the prudent advice of his most dear beloved Uncle, Edward, Duke of Somerset, Governor of his Majesty's person, and Protector of all his Highness's Realms, Dominions, and Subjects, with the rest of his most honourable Council.[1]

He has done so, most graciously considering the manifold scandals which before now have crept into his Grace's realm, through the false usurped power of the Bishop of Rome, and the ungodly doctrine of his adherents, not only to the great decay of Christian religion, but also (if God were not merciful) to the utter destruction of innumerable souls. These, through hypocrisy and harmful doctrine, were seduced and brought from honouring the only true, living, and eternal God, to the worshipping of creatures, indeed, of stocks and stones; from doing the commandments of God, to voluntary works and fantasies invented by humans; from true religion, to Popish superstition.[2]

These Homilies are set forth also considering the earnest and fervent desire of the King's dearly beloved subjects to be delivered from all errors and superstitions, and to be truly and faithfully instructed in the very word of God—that lively food of our souls—whereby they may learn unfeignedly and according to the mind of the Holy Spirit expressed in the scriptures, to honour God and to serve their King with all humility and subjection, and to behave

---

1   Edward Seymour (1506-1552), the brother of Henry VIII's third wife, Jane.

2   Voluntary works were those "above and beyond" our duties to love God and neighbour. This concept of "works of supererogation" is refuted in Article 14 of *The Thirty-nine Articles*.

themselves in a godly and honest way towards all.

Again, they are also set forth in remembrance that the next and most ready way to expel and avoid all corrupt, vicious, and ungodly living, as well as false doctrine tending to superstition and idolatry, and clearly to put away all contention which has before now arisen through diversity of preaching, is the true setting forth and pure declaring of God's word, which is the principal guide and leader to all godliness and virtue.

Finally, that all ministers, however learned they are, may have some godly and fruitful lessons in readiness, to read and declare unto their parishioners for their edifying, instruction, and comfort, the King has caused this book of *Homilies* to be made and set forth. In it is contained certain wholesome and godly exhortations, to move the people to honour and worship Almighty God and diligently to serve him, every one according to their degree, state, and vocation.

His Majesty commands and sincerely charges all Parsons, Vicars, Curates, and all others having spiritual cure, every Sunday in the year when the people are most gathered together, to read and declare these *Homilies* to their parishioners, plainly and distinctly, in such order as they stand in the book (unless any Sermon is preached, and then for that cause only and for none other, the reading of the said Homily is to be deferred unto the next Sunday following). And when this book of *Homilies* is read over, the King's Majesty's pleasure is that it should be repeated and read again, in such a way as was before prescribed, until such time as his Grace's pleasure shall further be known on this subject.

Also, his Majesty commands that the said ecclesiastical persons, upon the first holy day falling in the week time of every quarter of the year, shall read his injunctions openly and distinctly to the people, in manner and form in the same expressed.[3] And upon

---

3   The Royal Injunctions of 1547 were often bound together with the *Homilies*. They were concerned with, e.g. the observation of Lent, and rules against preaching without a license.

every other holy and feast day through the year, likewise falling in the week time, they shall recite the Paternoster [the Lord's Prayer], the articles of our faith [the Creed], and the Ten Commandments in English, openly before all the people, as in the said injunctions is specified—that all classes and all ages may learn to know God, and to serve him, according to his holy word.

AMEN.

THE READING OF
HOLY SCRIPTURE

For a Christian there can be nothing either more necessary
or profitable than the knowledge of holy scripture, since
in it is contained God's true word, setting forth his glory,
and also our duty. And there is no truth or doctrine necessary for
our justification and everlasting salvation except what is, or may
be, drawn out of that fountain and well of truth. Therefore, those
who desire to enter into the right and perfect way with God, must
apply their minds to know holy scripture, without which they can
neither sufficiently know God and his will, nor their office and
duty.

As drink is pleasant to those who are dry, and meat to those
who are hungry, so is the reading, hearing, searching, and studying
of holy scripture, to those who desire to know God, or themselves,
and to do his will. It is only those who are so drowned in worldly
vanities that they neither savour God nor any godliness, whose
stomachs loathe and abhor the heavenly knowledge and food of
God's word. Indeed, that is why they desire such vanities, rather
than the true knowledge of God.

When someone is sick of a fever, whatever they eat and drink,
however pleasant it is, is as bitter to them as wormwood—not
for the bitterness of the meat, but for the corruption and bitter-

---

* The original title of this Homily was *A Fruitful Exhortation to the Reading and Knowledge of Holy Scripture*.

ness that is in their own tongue and mouth. In the same way, the sweetness of God's word is bitter, not of itself, but only to those who have their minds corrupted by a long custom of sin and love of this world.

Therefore, forsaking the corrupt judgment of the fleshly, who care only for the wellbeing of their physical carcass, let us reverently hear and read holy scripture, which is the food of the soul (Matthew 4:4). Let us diligently search for the well of life in the books of the New and Old Testament, and not run to the stinking puddles of people's traditions, devised by human imagination, for our justification and salvation.

THE USEFULNESS OF SCRIPTURE

For in holy scripture is fully contained what we ought to do, and what to avoid, what to believe, what to love, and what to look for from God's hands. In these books we shall find the Father *from* whom, the Son *by* whom, and the Holy Spirit *in* whom, all things have their being and conservation; and these three Persons are but one God, and one substance.

In these books we may learn to know ourselves, how vile and pitiable we are; and also to know God, how good he is of himself, and how he makes us and all creatures partakers of his goodness. We may learn also in these books to know God's will and pleasure, as much as, for this present time, is convenient for us to know. And, as the great minister and godly preacher, St John Chrysostom, says, whatever is required for our salvation is fully contained in the scripture of God.[1]

Those who are ignorant, may there learn and have knowledge. Those who are hard-hearted, and obstinate sinners, shall there find everlasting torments, prepared by God's justice to make them

---

1   John Chrysostom (347-407) was Bishop of Constantinople in what is now Turkey. The quotation here is actually from Pseudo-Chrysostom's Homily 41 on Matthew's Gospel (PG 56:862) which omits the words "of God" at the end. See Thomas Oden (ed.), *Incomplete Commentary on Matthew* (translated by James Kellerman; Downers Grove: IVP, 2010).

afraid, and to mollify or soften them. The one who is oppressed with misery in this world, shall there find relief in the promises of everlasting life, to their great consolation and comfort. The one who is wounded (by the devil) unto death, shall find there medicine, by which they may be restored again to health.

If it is necessary to teach any truth, or reprove any false doctrine, to rebuke any vice, to commend any virtue, to give good counsel, to comfort, or to exhort, or to do any other thing necessary for our salvation—all those things (says St Chrysostom) we may learn plentifully from the scripture.[2] There is, says Fulgentius, abundantly enough, both for adults to eat, and children to suck—whatever is appropriate for all ages, and for all classes and sorts of people.[3]

These books, therefore, ought to be much in our hands, in our eyes, in our ears, in our mouths, but most of all in our hearts. For the scripture of God is heavenly meat for our souls (Matthew 4:4): the hearing and keeping of it makes us blessed (Luke 11:28), sanctifies us (John 17:17), and makes us holy; it converts our souls (Psalm 19:7); it is a light lantern to our feet (Psalm 119:105, 130); it is a sure, steadfast, and everlasting instrument of salvation; it gives wisdom to the humble and lowly hearts (Luke 10:39 42); it comforts, makes glad, cheers, and cherishes our conscience; it is a more excellent jewel, or treasure, than any gold or precious stone (Psalm 19:10); it is more sweet than honey or honeycomb (Psalm 119:103); it is called the best part, which Mary chose (Luke 10:42); for it has in it everlasting comfort.

---

2   John Chrysostom's Homily on 2 Timothy 3:16-17 (PG 65:721; NPNF 13:510).

3   Fulgentius (462-533) was Bishop of Ruspe in what is now Tunisia. The reference is to his first sermon *On the Stewards of the Lord* (PL 65:721). Gregory the Great (539-604) also speaks of the word of God as feeding both children and the wise, and as like a river, shallow enough for a lamb to paddle in, while deep enough also for an elephant to swim. See his *Moralia in Job*, Epistle to Leander §4 (PL 76:515), also in *Moral Reflections on the Book of Job* (trans. Brian Kerns; Collegville, Minnesota: Liturgical Press, 2014), 1.53.

THE POWER OF SCRIPTURE

The words of holy scripture are called words of everlasting life (John 6:68), for they are God's instrument, ordained for that purpose. They have power to convert, through God's promise and they are effectual through God's assistance. Being received in a faithful heart, they always have a heavenly spiritual working in them (Colossians 1:5-6, 25-28). They are lively, active, and mighty in operation, and sharper than any two-edged sword, penetrating even to dividing soul and spirit, joints and marrow (Hebrews 4:12).

Christ calls them wise builders, who build upon his word, upon his sure and substantial foundation (Matthew 7:24). By this word of God we shall be judged: for the word that I speak, says Christ, shall judge on the last day (John 12:48). The one who keeps the word of Christ is promised the love and favour of God, and that they shall be the dwelling-place or temple of the blessed Trinity. Great affection for the temporary things of this world shall be diminished in whoever is diligent to read this word, and in their heart to print what they read. And great desire for heavenly things that are promised by God in it, shall increase in them.

There is nothing that so much strengthens our faith and trust in God, that so much keeps up innocence and purity of heart, and also of outward godly life and conversation, as continual reading and meditation on God's word. For that thing which (by perpetual reading of holy scripture, and diligent searching of the same) is deeply imprinted and engraved on the heart, at length turns almost into nature. And, moreover, the effect and virtue of God's word is to illuminate the ignorant, and to give more light to those who faithfully and diligently read it; to comfort their hearts, and to encourage them to perform that which is commanded by God. It teaches them patience in all adversity, and in prosperity it teaches humility. It teaches what honour is due to God, and what mercy and charity is due to our neighbour. It gives good counsel in all doubtful things. It shows to whom we shall look for aid and help in all perils; and that God is the only giver of victory in all battles and temptations, bodily and spiritual (1 Samuel 14:6-23; 2 Chronicles 20:1-30; 1 Corinthians 15:57; 1 John 5:4).

In reading of God's word, it is not the one who is most eager to turn the pages or who recites it from memory who profits the most. Rather, it is the one who is most turned to God by it, the one who is most inspired with the Holy Spirit, most in their heart and life altered and changed into that thing which they read—the one who is daily less and less proud, less wrathful, less covetous, and less desirous of worldly and vain pleasures—who daily forsaking their old life of vice, increase in virtue more and more.

In short, there is nothing that more maintains godliness of the mind, and drives away ungodliness, than continual reading or hearing of God's word, if it is joined with a godly mind, and a good affection to know and follow God's will. For without a single eye, pure intent, and good mind, nothing is counted as good before God. And, on the other side, nothing more darkens Christ and the glory of God, nor brings in more blindness and all kinds of vices, than does ignorance of God's word (Isaiah 5:13, 24; Matthew 22:29; 1 Corinthians 14).

THE MOST IMPORTANT SCIENCE

In the first part of this sermon, which exhorts us to the knowledge of holy scripture, it was declared how the knowledge of scripture is necessary and profitable to all; and that, by the true knowledge and understanding of scripture, the most necessary points of our duty towards God and our neighbours are also known. Now, concerning the same matter, you shall hear what follows.

IGNORANCE OF SCRIPTURE

If we profess Christ, why are we not ashamed to be ignorant of his doctrine, seeing that everyone is ashamed to be ignorant in that learning which they profess? Someone who does not read books of philosophy is ashamed to be called a Philosopher; or to be called a Lawyer, an Astronomer, or a Physician, if they are ignorant in the books of law, astronomy, and medicine. How can anyone, then, say that they profess Christ and his religion, if they will not apply themselves as far as they conveniently can to read and hear, and so to know, the books of Christ's gospel and doctrine?

Although other sciences are good, and to be learned, yet no one can deny that this is the chief science, which passes all others incomparably. What excuse shall we therefore make at the last day before Christ, if we delight to read or hear human fantasies and inventions more than his most holy gospel, and will find no time to do that which chiefly above all things we should do? What excuse is there if we would rather read other things than that, for which we ought to drop every other book? Let us who profess God and have faith and trust in him, therefore, apply ourselves, as far as we can have time and leisure, to know God's word, by diligent hearing and reading of it.

But those who have no good affection for God's word commonly allege two vain and feigned excuses, to colour this their fault. Some try to excuse themselves by their own frailty and fearfulness, saying that they dare not read holy scripture, in case through their ignorance they should fall into any error. Others pretend that the difficulty of understanding it, and the hardness of it, is so great that it is only appropriate for clergy and learned people to read it.

FEAR OF ERROR

As touching the first: ignorance of God's word is the cause of all error; as Christ himself affirmed to the Sadducees, saying that they were mistaken because they did not know the scripture (Matthew 22:29). How then should those who wish still to be ignorant ever avoid error? And how should they come out of ignorance, if they will not read nor hear that thing which would give them knowledge? The one who now has most knowledge, was ignorant to begin with; yet they did not abstain from reading for fear that they should fall into error. So, for the same reason, you may as well lie still and never go anywhere, in case if you go, you fall into a swamp; nor eat any good meat, in case you eat too much; nor sow your corn, nor labour in your occupation, nor use your merchandise, for fear you may lose your seed, your labour, your stock. And so, by that reasoning, it would be best for you to live idly, and never to take it in hand to do any manner of good thing, in case perhaps some evil thing may happen because of it.

If you are afraid to fall into error by reading holy scripture, I shall show you how you may read it without danger of error. Read it humbly, with a meek and lowly heart, to the intent that you may glorify God, and not yourself, with the knowledge of it. And read it not without daily praying to God, that he would direct your reading to good effect. And take upon you to expound it no further than you can plainly understand it. For, as St Augustine says, the knowledge of holy scripture is a great, large, and high place; but the door is very low, so that the high and arrogant person cannot run in; but must stoop low, and humble themselves, in order to enter into it.[4]

Presumption and arrogance is the mother of all error; and humility needs to fear no error. For humility will only search to know the truth: it will search and will bring together one place with another; and where it cannot find out the meaning, it will pray, it will ask others who know, and will not presumptuously and rashly define any thing which it does not know. Therefore, the humble may search any truth boldly in the scripture, without any danger of error. And if they are ignorant, they ought all the more to read and search holy scripture, to bring them out of ignorance. A person may profit by only hearing of the word; but they may much more profit with both hearing and reading.

---

4 Augustine (354-430) was Bishop of Hippo in what is now Algeria. The reference is to his book *The Confessions* Book 3 Chapter 5 (PL 32:686; NPNF 1:62), and/ or his Sermon 51, Section 6 (PL 38:336; NPNF 5:247).

The First Book of Homilies

THE DIFFICULTY OF SCRIPTURE

I have said this regarding those who are afraid to read, because they are ignorant. But concerning the hardness of scripture, I say this: those who are so weak that they are not able to tolerate strong meat, they may still suck the sweet and tender milk and defer the rest until they grow stronger, and come to more knowledge (1 Corinthians 3:2; Hebrews 5:12-14). For God receives the learned and unlearned, and casts away none, but is impartial to all. And the scripture is full of low valleys, plain and easy ways for everyone to use and to walk in, as well as of high hills and mountains, which few can climb up. As St John Chrysostom says:

> "Whoever gives their mind to the holy scriptures with diligent study and burning desire, it cannot be that they should be left without help. For either God Almighty will send them some godly Doctor to teach them—as he did to instruct the Eunuch, a noble-man of Ethiopia, and treasurer to Queen Candace (Acts 8:26-35); who having a great affection to read the scripture, although he did not understood it, yet, for the desire that he had for God's word, God sent his apostle Philip to declare to him the true sense of the scripture that he read. Or, on the other hand, if we lack someone learned to instruct and teach us, yet God himself from above will give light to our minds, and teach us those things which are necessary for us, and in which we are ignorant."[5]

In another place, Chrysostom says that our "human and worldly wisdom, or science, is not necessary for the understanding of scripture; but the revelation of the Holy Spirit, who reveals the true meaning to those who with humility and diligence search for it."[6] The one who asks shall have, and the one who seeks shall find, and the one who knocks shall have the door opened (Matthew 7:8). If we read once, twice, or three times, and still do not

---

5   Chrysostom, Homily 35 on Genesis. See Saint John Chrysostom, *Homilies on Genesis 18-45* (translated by Robert Hill; Washington: Catholic University of America Press, 1990), 304-305 (PG 53:321).

6   Chrysostom, Homily 21 on Genesis. See Chrysostom, *Homilies in Genesis 18-45*, 51 (PG 53:175).

understand, let us not cease to read; but still continue reading, praying, asking others. And so, by continual knocking, eventually the door shall be opened, as St Augustine says.[7]

Although many things in scripture are spoken in obscure or mysterious ways, there is nothing which is spoken under dark mysteries in one place, which is not also spoken about more familiarly and plainly in other places, to suit the capacity both of the educated and the uneducated.[8] And everyone's duty is to learn those things in the scripture that are plain to understand and necessary for salvation, to print them in memory and effectually to exercise them; and, as for the dark mysteries, to be content to be ignorant in them, until such time as it shall please God to open those things to us.

In the meantime, if we lack either aptitude or opportunity, God will not put that down to our folly. Nevertheless, it is not fitting that those who are able to read should set aside reading because some others cannot. Nevertheless, we ought not to neglect reading of the whole simply because some places are hard. And briefly to conclude: as St Augustine says, "by the scripture all are amended; the weak are strengthened, and the strong are comforted."[9] So that surely none are enemies to the reading of God's word, except those who are ignorant, and do not know how wholesome a thing it is; or those who are so sick, that they hate the most effective medicine that would heal them; or so ungodly, that they would wish the people still to continue in blindness and ignorance of God.

Thus we have briefly touched on some of the attributes of God's holy word, which is one of God's chief and principal benefits, given and declared to mankind here on earth. Let us thank God

---

7   Augustine, Sermon 270, on the day of Pentecost. See John Rotelle (ed.), *Sermons III/7 (230-272B) on the Liturgical Seasons* (translated by Edmund Hill; New Rochelle, NY: New City Press, 1993), 288 (PL 38:1237-1238).

8   Augustine, *On Christian Doctrine*, Book 2, Chapter 6[8] (PL 34:39; NPNF 2:537).

9   Augustine, Epistle 137, Section 18 (PL 33:524; NPNF 1:480).

heartily for this, his great and special gift, beneficial favour, and fatherly providence. Let us be glad to fan into flame this precious gift of our heavenly Father (2 Timothy 1:6). Let us hear, read, and know these holy rules, injunctions, and statutes of our Christian religion, of which we have made profession to God at our baptism. Let us with fear and reverence lay up, in the treasure chest of our hearts, these necessary and fruitful lessons. Let us, night and day, muse and meditate on and contemplate them (Psalm 1:2). Let us ruminate and, as it were, chew the cud like a cow, that we may have the sweet juice, spiritual effect, marrow, honey, kernel, taste, comfort and consolation of them. Let us ponder, quietly, and certify our consciences with the most infallible certainty, truth, and perpetual assurance of them.

And let us pray to God, the only Author of these heavenly studies, that we may speak, think, believe, live, and depart hence, according to the wholesome doctrine and truths of them. And, by that means, in this world we shall have God's defence, favour, and grace, with the unspeakable solace of peace, and quietness of conscience; and, after this pitiable life, we shall enjoy the endless bliss and glory of heaven: which, may he grant to us all, who died for us all, Jesus Christ: to whom, with the Father and the Holy Spirit, be all honour and glory, both now and everlastingly. *Amen.*

THE MISERY OF ALL MANKIND

T he Holy Spirit, in writing the holy scripture, is in nothing more diligent than to pull down our vainglory and pride, which of all vices is most universally grafted into all mankind, even from the first infection of our first father Adam. And therefore we read, in many places of scripture, many notable lessons against this old rooted vice, to teach us the most commendable virtue of humility, how to know ourselves, and to remember what we are of ourselves.

DUST AND ASHES

In the book of Genesis, Almighty God gives us all a title and name in our great grandfather Adam, which ought to warn us all to consider what we are, where we came from, and where we shall go. He says, "By the sweat of your brow you shall eat bread, until you return to the ground, for out of it you were taken; for you are dust, and to dust you shall return" (Genesis 3:19). Here, as it were, in a mirror we may learn to know ourselves, that we are but ground, earth, and ashes, and that to earth and ashes we shall return.

Also, the holy Patriarch Abraham well remembered this name and title—dust, earth, and ashes—appointed and assigned by God to all mankind. That is why he calls himself by that name when

---

* The original title of this Homily was *A Homily of the Misery of All Mankind and of their Condemnation to Death Everlasting, by Their Own Sin.*

he makes his earnest prayer for Sodom and Gomorrah (Genesis 18:27). And we read that Judith,[1] Esther (Esther 14:2), Job (Job 42:6), Jeremiah (Jeremiah 6:26, 25:34), with other holy men and women in the Old Testament, used sackcloth, and cast dust and ashes upon their heads when they lamented their sinful living. They called and cried to God, for help and mercy, with such a ceremony of sackcloth, dust, and ashes, that they might declare by this, to the whole world, what a humble and lowly estimation they had of themselves, and how well they remembered their previously mentioned name and title, their vile, corrupt, frail nature—dust, earth, and ashes.

The book of Wisdom,[2] also willing to pull down our proud hearts, moves us diligently to remember our mortal and earthly origins. It says we all come from the one who was first made, and that all of us, kings as well as subjects, come into this world and go out of it in the same way—that is, of ourselves totally pitiable, as we may daily see. And Almighty God commanded his Prophet Isaiah to make a proclamation, and cry to the whole world. And Isaiah, asking, "What shall I cry?", the Lord answered, "Cry, that all flesh is grass, and that all its glory is like the flower of the field. The grass withers and the flower falls, when the wind of the LORD blows upon it. Surely the people are grass, which dries up, and the flower fades away" (Isaiah 40:6-7).

And the holy man Job, having in himself great experience of the miserable and sinful state of man, reveals the same to the world in these words: "Mortals, born of a woman, are few of days and full of trouble. They spring up like flowers and then wither away; like fleeting shadows, they do not last. Do you fix your eyes on them? Will you bring me into judgment with you? Who can bring

---

1   See the apocryphal book of Judith 4:10-11, 9:1. As the *Thirty-nine Articles* (Article 6) say, these additional books are not part of holy scripture as such, yet may be read "for example of life and instruction of manners", although the church "does not apply them to establish any doctrine."

2   From the apocryphal book of The Wisdom of Solomon (not the Old Testament book of Proverbs): Wisdom 7:1-6.

what is pure out of something impure?" (Job 14:1-4). And all people, in their evilness and natural inclinations, are so universally given to sin, that (as the scripture says) "God regretted that ever he made them" (Genesis 6:6). And his indignation was so much provoked against the world by sin, that he drowned all the world with Noah's flood, except Noah himself, and his little household (Genesis 7).

It is not without great cause, that the scripture of God so many times calls all people here in this world by this word, "earth". "O earth, earth, earth," says Jeremiah, "Hear the word of the LORD!" (Jeremiah 22:29). This, our right name, calling, and title—"earth, earth, earth"—pronounced by the Prophet, shows what we truly are, regardless of whatever other honours, titles, or dignities people may use of us. This is what he who knows us best (both what we are and what we ought rightly to be called) plainly named us.

ALL ARE SINNERS
And this is how he describes us, speaking by his faithful apostle, St Paul: "Jews and Greeks alike are all under sin. As it is written: There is no one righteous, not even one; there is no one who understands; no one who seeks for God. All have turned away, and have together become worthless; there is no one who does good, not even one. Their throats are open graves; their tongues practice deception. The venom of vipers is on their lips. Their mouths are full of curses and bitterness. Their feet are swift to shed blood; ruin and misery are in their paths, and the way of peace they do not know. There is no fear of God before their eyes" (Romans 3:9-18). And in another place, St Paul writes in this way: "God has bound everyone over to disobedience so that he may have mercy on all of them" (Romans 11:32).

The scripture locks up all under sin, so that the promise that is given through faith in Jesus Christ, should be given to those who believe (Galatians 3:22). St Paul in many places paints us in our true colours, calling us the children of the wrath of God when we are born (Ephesians 2:3), saying also that we cannot think a good thought of ourselves, much less can we say well, or do well of ourselves (2 Corinthians 3:5). And the wise man says in the book of Proverbs, "the righteous fall seven times a day" (Proverbs 24:16). The most tried and approved man Job, feared all his works (Job 9:28).[3] St John the Baptist was sanctified in his mother's womb, and praised before he was born. He was called an Angel, and great before the Lord, filled even from his birth with the Holy Spirit, the preparer of the way for our Saviour Christ, and commended by our Saviour Christ to be more than a Prophet, and the greatest that ever was born of a woman (Luke 1:15, 76, Malachi 3:1, Matthew 11:9-11). Yet he plainly grants that he needed to be washed by Christ. He worthily praised and glorified his Lord and master Christ, and humbled himself as unworthy to unbuckle his shoes, giving all honour and glory to God (Matthew 3:11-14).

So does St Paul both often and evidently confess that he was, of himself, ever giving (as a most faithful servant) all praise to his master and Saviour. So does blessed St John the Evangelist, in the name of himself and of all other holy men (be they never so just) make this open confession: "If we say we have no sin, we deceive ourselves, and the truth is not in us. If we acknowledge our sins, God is faithful and just to forgive our sins and to cleanse us from all unrighteousness. If we say we have not sinned, we make him a liar, and his word is not in us" (1 John 1:8-10).

For this reason, the wise man in the book called Ecclesiastes makes this true and general confession, "There is no one on the earth who is so righteous that they do good and never sin" (Ecclesiastes 7:20). David is ashamed of his sin, but not ashamed to confess it (Psalm 51). How often, how earnestly, he laments and desires God's great mercy for his great offences, and that God should not enter into judgment with him (Psalm 143:2)! And again, how

---

3   Most English translations, agreeing with the Hebrew text, say Job feared all his sufferings or sorrows (KJV, NIV, ESV, NRSV). The Homily here is alluding to the Latin Vulgate which says Job feared all his works.

well does this holy man weigh his sins, when he confesses that they are so many in number, and so hidden and hard to understand, that it is in a manner impossible to know, utter, or number them (Psalm 19:12, 40:12). This is why he, having a true, earnest, and deep contemplation and consideration of his sins, and yet not coming to the bottom of them, he makes supplication to God to forgive him his private, secret, hidden sins which we cannot know. He rightly weighs his sins from the original root and headspring, perceiving inclinations, provocations, stirrings, stingings, buds, branches, dregs, infections, tastes, feelings, and scents of them to continue in him still. So he says, "Behold, I was conceived in sins" (Psalm 51:5)—out of one (like a fountain) all the rest spring.[4]

LAY DOWN YOUR PRIDE

Our Saviour Christ says, "No one is good except God alone" (Luke 18:19), and that we can do nothing that is good without him (John 15:5). Nor can anyone come to the Father but by him (John 14:6). He commands us also to say that we are un-profitable servants, when we have done all that we can do (Luke 17:10). He prefers the penitent tax collector, before the proud, holy, and glorious Pharisee (Luke 18:9-14). He calls himself a Doctor (Matthew 9:12), not for those who are whole, but for those who are sick and have need of his salve for their sore.

He teaches us in our prayers to acknowledge ourselves sinners, and to ask for righteousness and deliverance from all evils, from our heavenly Father's hand. He declares that the sins of our own hearts defile our own selves (Mark 7:14-23). He teaches that an evil word or thought deserves condemnation, affirming that we shall give account for every idle word (Matthew 12:36). He says he came to save none but the sheep that were utterly lost, and cast

---

4   Again, the Homily relies on the Latin Vulgate here, which has "sins" plural, whereas English translations, following the Hebrew, now have "sin" in the singular (KJV, ESV). But as Calvin comments on this verse, David here acknowledges that he "had been born into the world with the seed of every iniquity."

away (Matthew 15:24).

Therefore few of the proud, just, learned, wise, perfect, and holy Pharisees were saved by him, because they justified themselves by their counterfeit holiness before people. Therefore (good people) let us beware of such hypocrisy, vainglory, and justifying of ourselves. Let us look down at our feet, and then down peacock's feathers, down proud heart, down vile clay, frail and brittle vessels!

Our Sinful Inability

Since true knowledge of ourselves is very necessary to come to the right knowledge of God, you have heard in the last homily how humbly all godly people have always thought of themselves. They are taught to think and judge of themselves this way by God their Creator in his holy word. For of ourselves we are crabtrees, that can bring forth no apples. We are of ourselves of such earth as can bring forth only weeds, nettles, brambles, briers, corncockle, and darnel.

Our imperfect fruit

Our fruits are declared in the fifth chapter of Galatians. We have neither faith, charity, hope, patience, chastity, nor anything else that is good, except from God, and therefore these virtues are called there "the fruit of the Spirit", and not the fruit of mankind (Galatians 5:19-23). Let us therefore acknowledge ourselves before God to be pitiable and wretched sinners (as indeed we are). And let us earnestly repent, and humble ourselves heartily, and cry to God for mercy. Let us all confess with mouth and heart, that we are full of imperfections. Let us know our own works, how imperfect they are, and then we shall not stand foolishly and arrogantly in our own conceits, nor think we can obtain justification by our merits or works.

For truly there are imperfections in our best works. We do not love God so much as we are bound to do, with all our heart, mind, and power. We do not fear God so much as we ought to do. We do not pray to God, but with great and many imperfections. We give, forgive, believe, live, and hope imperfectly. We speak, think, and do imperfectly. We fight against the devil, the world, and the flesh imperfectly. Let us therefore not be ashamed to confess plainly our state of imperfection; indeed, let us not be ashamed to confess imperfection, even in all our best works.

Let none of us be ashamed to say with holy St Peter, "I am a sinful man!" (Luke 5:8). Let us say with the holy Prophet David, "We have sinned like our fathers; we have done wrong and acted wickedly" (Psalm 106:6). Let us all make open confession with the prodigal son to our father, and say with him, "We have sinned against heaven, and against you (O Father). We are not worthy to be called your children" (Luke 15:18-19). Let us all say with holy Baruch, "O Lord our God, to us is worthily ascribed shame and confusion, and to you righteousness. We have sinned, we have done wickedly, we have acted unrighteously in all your commands".[5] Let us all say with the holy Prophet Daniel, "O Lord, righteousness belongs to you, but to us belongs confusion. We have sinned, we have committed iniquity, we have offended. We have fled from you, and departed from all your precepts and judgments" (Daniel 9:7, 5). So we learn of all good people in holy scriptures, to humble ourselves, and to exalt, extol, praise, magnify, and glorify God.

OUR NEED OF MERCY

Thus we have heard how evil we are of ourselves—how of ourselves, and by ourselves, we have no goodness, help, nor salvation. On the contrary, we have sin, damnation, and death everlasting. If we deeply weigh and consider this, we shall better understand the great mercy of God, and how our salvation comes only by Christ. For in and of ourselves, we find nothing by which we may be deliv-

---

5   From the book of Baruch 2:6, 12, in the Apocrypha. See the first footnote in this chapter, on the Anglican view of these inter-testamental books.

ered from this miserable captivity (2 Corinthians 3:5), into which we were cast through the envy of the devil, by transgressing God's commandment in our first parent Adam. We have all become unclean (Psalm 51:1-10), but none of us are able to cleanse ourselves, nor to make each other clean. We are by nature the children of God's wrath, but we are not able to make ourselves the children and inheritors of God's glory (Ephesians 2:3).

We are sheep that have gone astray (1 Peter 2:25), but we cannot by our own power come again to the sheepfold, so great is our imperfection and weakness. In ourselves, therefore, we may not glory, since of ourselves we are nothing but sinful. Neither may we rejoice in any works that we do, which are all so imperfect and impure that they are not able to stand before the righteous throne of God, as the holy Prophet David says, "Enter not into judgment with your servant (O Lord), for no one living shall be found righteous in your sight" (Psalm 143:2). To God therefore we must flee, or else we shall never find peace, rest, and quietness of conscience in our hearts.

For he is the Father of mercies and God of all consolation (2 Corinthians 1:3). He is the Lord, with whom is plenteous redemption (Psalm 130:7). He is the God who of his own mercy saves us, and sets out his charity and exceeding love towards us (Titus 3:5; Romans 5:8). Of his own voluntary goodness, when we were dead, he saved us, and provided an everlasting kingdom for us. And all these heavenly treasures are given us, not for our own deserts, merits, or good deeds (which of ourselves we do not have) but of his mere mercy, freely.

SAVED IN CHRIST ALONE

And for whose sake? Truly it is for Jesus Christ's sake, that pure and undefiled lamb of God (1 Peter 1:19). He is that dearly beloved Son, for whose sake God is fully pacified, satisfied, and set at one with man. He is the Lamb of God who takes away the sins of the world (John 1:29), of whom only it may be truly spoken, that he did all things well (Mark 7:37), and in his mouth was found no deceit or guile (1 Peter 2:22). None but he alone may say, "The prince of this world is coming but he has no hold on me" (John 14:30). And he alone may also say, "Which of you shall prove me guilty of any fault?" (John 8:46) He is the high and everlasting Priest, who has offered himself once-and-for-all upon the altar of the cross and with that one offering has made perfect for evermore those who are sanctified (Hebrews 7:24-27, 10:14, 13:10). He is the only mediator between God and mankind (1 Timothy 2:5-6), who paid our ransom to God with his own blood (Revelation 5:9, 1:5), and with that has cleansed us all from sin (1 John 1:7). He is the Doctor who heals all our diseases (Psalm 103:3). He is that Saviour who saves his people from all their sins (Matthew 1:21).

To be short, he is that flowing and most plenteous fountain, of whose fulness all we have received (John 1:16). For in him alone are all the treasures of the wisdom and knowledge of God hidden (Colossians 2:3). And in him, and by him, we have from God the Father all good things, whether of the body or the soul (Romans 8:32). O how much are we bound to this our heavenly Father for his great mercies, which he has so plenteously declared to us in Christ Jesus our Lord and Saviour! What worthy and sufficient thanks can we give to him? Let us all with one accord burst out with joyful voice, ever praising and magnifying this Lord of mercy, for his tender kindness shown to us in his dearly beloved Son, Jesus Christ our Lord.

So far, we have heard what we are of ourselves: truly sinful, wretched, and damnable. Again, we have heard how of ourselves, and by ourselves, we are not able either to think a good thought or work a good deed, so that we can find in ourselves no hope of salvation, but rather whatever makes for our destruction. Again, we have heard of the tender kindness and great mercy of God the Father towards us, and how beneficial he is to us for Christ's sake, without our merits or deserts, even of his own mere mercy and tender goodness.

Now, how these exceedingly great mercies of God, spread abroad in Christ Jesus for us, are obtained, and how we are delivered from the captivity of sin, death, and hell, it shall (with God's help) be further declared in the next Homily. In the meantime— indeed, at all times—let us learn to know ourselves, our frailty and weakness, without any ostentation or boasting of our own good deeds and merits. Let us also acknowledge the exceeding mercy of God towards us, and confess that just as from ourselves comes all evil and damnation, so likewise of him comes all goodness and salvation, as God himself says by the Prophet Hosea, "O Israel, you are destroyed, in me only is your help and comfort" (Hosea 13:9).

If we thus humbly submit ourselves in the sight of God, we may be sure that on the day of judgment he will lift us up to the kingdom of his dearly beloved Son, Christ Jesus our Lord—to whom, with the Father, and the Holy Spirit, be all honour and glory for ever. Amen.

HOMILY 3

SALVATION BY
CHRIST ALONE

Because all people are sinners and offenders against God, and breakers of his law and commandments, therefore no one can, by their own acts, works, and deeds (however good they seem) be justified, and made righteous before God. Everyone of necessity is constrained to seek for another righteousness or justification, to be received from God's own hands—that is to say, the cancellation, pardon, and forgiveness of their sins and trespasses, in such things as they have offended. And this justification or righteousness, which we receive by God's mercy and Christ's merits embraced by faith, is taken, accepted, and counted by God as our perfect and full justification.

THE JUSTICE AND MERCY OF GOD
In order to understand this more fully, it is our part and duty always to remember the great mercy of God. When all the world was wrapped in sin by breaking of the Law, God sent his only son, our Saviour Christ, into this world to fulfil the Law for us. By shedding his most precious blood, he made a sacrifice and satisfaction, or (as we might say) he made amends to his Father for our sins, to satisfy the wrath and indignation he had against us for them.

---

* The original title of this Homily was *A Homily of the Salvation of Mankind Only by Christ our Saviour from Sin and Death Everlasting.*

Infants, being baptised and dying in their infancy, are by this sacrifice washed from their sins, brought to God's favour, and made his children, and inheritors of his kingdom of heaven. And those who sin after their baptism, in act or deed, when they convert and sincerely turn again to God, they are likewise washed by this sacrifice from their sins, in such a way that there remains no spot of sin that shall be imputed to their damnation. This is that justification or righteousness which St Paul speaks of when he says "No one is justified by the works of the Law, but freely by faith in Jesus Christ" (Romans 3:20-24). And again he says, "We believe in Jesus Christ, so that we may be justified freely by faith in Christ, and not by the works of the Law, because that no one shall be justified by the works of the Law" (Galatians 2:16).

Although this justification is free for us, it does not come so freely to us that there is therefore no ransom paid at all. But here, our reasoning may be confused, if we reason in this fashion: if a ransom is paid for our redemption, then it is not given to us freely. For a prisoner who paid their ransom is not let go freely; for if they go freely, then they go without ransom—for what else is it to go freely, than to be set at liberty without paying a ransom? This argument is answered by the great wisdom of God in this mystery of our redemption. He has so tempered his justice and mercy together that he would neither, by his justice, condemn us to the everlasting captivity of the devil, and his prison of Hell, remediless for ever without mercy—nor, by his mercy, deliver us without justice or payment of a just ransom. Rather, to his endless mercy he joined his most upright and equal justice.

He has shown us his great mercy in delivering us from our former captivity, without requiring any ransom to be paid, or amends to be made by us, which it would have been impossible for us to do. And since we did not have it in us to do so, he provided a ransom for us—the most precious body and blood of his own most dear and best beloved son Jesus Christ who, besides his ransom, fulfilled the Law for us perfectly. And so the justice of God, and his mercy embraced each other, and fulfilled the mystery of our redemption.

St Paul speaks of this justice and mercy of God knit together in Romans 3. "All have offended, and fallen short of the glory of God, but are justified freely by his grace, by the redemption which is in Jesus Christ, whom God has presented to us as a reconciler and peacemaker, through faith in his blood, to show his righteousness" (Romans 3:23-25). And in Romans 10, "Christ is the end of the law for righteousness, to everyone who believes" (Romans 10:4). And in Romans 8, "For what the law was powerless to do because it was weakened by the flesh, God himself did by sending his own Son in the likeness of sinful flesh to be a sin offering. He condemned sin in the flesh, in order that the righteous requirement of the law might be fulfilled in us, who do not walk according to the flesh but according to the Spirit" (Romans 8:3-4).

Not by our good works

In these places, the apostle especially touches three things, which must concur and go together in our justification: on God's part, his great mercy and grace; on Christ's part, justice, that is, the satisfaction of God's justice, or the price of our redemption by the offering of his body and shedding of his blood, with fulfilling of the law perfectly and thoroughly; and on our part, true and lively faith in the merits of Jesus Christ, which yet is not ours, but comes by God's working in us. So in our justification, we find not only God's mercy and grace, but also his justice, which the apostle calls "the justice of God" (Romans 3:21-22, 25-26), and which consists in paying our ransom, and fulfilling the Law. So the grace of God does not exclude the justice of God in our justification, but only excludes human justice, that is to say, the righteousness of our works, as if they could be meritorious and earn our justification.

Therefore, St Paul declares here nothing on our part, concerning our justification, but only a true and lively faith, which nevertheless is the gift of God, and not our work alone, without God.

And yet that faith does not exclude repentance, hope, love, dread, and the fear of God, to be joined with faith in everyone who is justified. But it does exclude them from the role of justifying. So that although they are all present together in the one who is justified, yet they do not themselves justify us.

Nor does faith exclude the righteousness of our good works, which are necessarily to be done afterwards out of duty towards God. For we are very much bound to serve God, in doing good deeds, commanded by him in his holy scripture, all the days of our life. But it excludes them in the sense that we may not do them with this intent: to be made good by doing them. For all the good works that we can do are imperfect, and therefore not able to deserve our justification. But our justification comes freely by the mere mercy of God, and of such great and free mercy that whereas no-one in the world was able of themselves to pay any part towards their ransom, it pleased our heavenly Father of his infinite mercy, without us deserving any of it, to prepare for us the most precious jewels of Christ's body and blood, whereby our ransom might be fully paid, the Law fulfilled, and his justice fully satisfied. So that Christ is now the righteousness of all those who truly believe in him. He, for them, paid their ransom by his death. He, for them, fulfilled the Law in his life. So that now in him, and by him, every true Christian may be called a fulfiller of the Law, because that which their infirmity lacked, Christ's justice has supplied.

THE ANCIENT DOCTRINE OF JUSTIFICATION

You have heard that everyone should seek for their justification and righteousness from Christ, and how also this righteousness comes to us by Christ's death and merits. You heard also that three things are required to obtain our righteousness, that is, God's mercy, Christ's justice, and a true and living faith (out of which springs good works). Also it has been declared at length that no one can be justified by their own good works, and that no one fulfils the Law according to the full demands of the Law.

St Paul in his Epistle to the Galatians proves the same, saying "If there had been any law given which could have justified, truly righteousness would have been by the law" (Galatians 3:21). And again he says, "If righteousness is by the Law, then Christ died in vain" (Galatians 2:21). And again he says, "You who are justified by the Law, have fallen away from grace" (Galatians 5:4). And furthermore, he writes to the Ephesians in this way: "By grace you are saved, through faith, and that not of yourselves, for it is the gift of God, and not of works, in case anyone should boast" (Ephesians 2:8-9). In short, the sum of all Paul's argument is this: that if justification comes by works, then it does not come by grace; and if it comes by grace, then it does not come by works. And to this end tend all the Prophets, as St Peter says in Acts 10: "All the prophets testify about Christ that through his name, all those who believe in him shall receive the cancellation of sins" (Acts 10:43).

FAITH ALONE IN THE EARLY CHURCH

In the same way, all the old and ancient authors, writing in both Greek and Latin, speak about being justified only by this true and living faith in Christ.[1] Of these, I will especially go through three: Hilary, Basil, and Ambrose. St Hilary says these words plainly in the ninth Canon on Matthew, "Faith alone justifies."[2] And St Basil, a Greek author, writes thus: "This is a perfect and a whole rejoicing in God: when someone does not advance themselves for their own righteousness, but acknowledges themselves

---

1 Amongst Cranmer's papers, there is a document called "Notes on Justification" in his handwriting, which includes a great many quotations "from Scripture, the Fathers, and the Schoolmen" on the subject of justification by faith *alone* and the idea that justification must precede good works. See J. E. Cox (ed.), *Miscellaneous Writings and Letters of Thomas Cranmer* (Cambridge: Cambridge University Press, 1846), 203-211. There is another helpful collection of such testimonies in George Downame, *A Treatise of Justification* (1633), 376-388.

2 Hilary (314-366) was Bishop of Poitiers in France. The reference is to his book *In Evangelium Matthaei*, Chapter 8, Section 6. See St Hilary of Poitiers, *Commentary on Matthew* (translated by D. H. Williams; Washington: Catholic University of America Press, 2012), 101 (PL 9:961).

to lack true justice and righteousness, and to be justified by faith alone in Christ." And Paul, he says, "glories in the contempt of his own righteousness, and looks for his righteousness from God, by faith."[3] These are the very words of St Basil. And St Ambrose, a Latin Author, says these words, "This is the ordinance of God, that those who believe in Christ should be saved without works, by faith only, freely receiving cancellation of their sins."[4] Consider diligently these words: without works, by faith only, freely we receive cancellation of our sins. What can be spoken more plainly, than to say that freely without works, by faith only, we obtain cancellation of our sins?

These and other similar sentences, that we are justified by faith only, freely, and without works, we often read in the best and most ancient writers. Besides Hilary, Basil, and St Ambrose as mentioned before, we read the same in Origen,[5] St Chrysostom,[6] St Cyprian,[7]

---

3   Basil (328-378) was Bishop of Caesarea Mazaca in Cappadocia, in what is now Turkey. The reference is to his *Sermon on Humility*, Homily 20, Section 3. See Saint Basil, *Ascetical Works* (translated by M. Monica Wagner; Washington: Catholic University of America Press, 1962), 479 (PG 31:529/30).

4   Ambrose (339-397) was Bishop of Milan in Italy. The quotation is actually from a commentary on 1 Corinthians (1:4) which circulated alongside the works of Ambrose during the middle ages and so is often said to be by Ambrosiaster ("Star of Ambrose"), although their true identity is disputed. See Ambrosiaster, *Commentaries on Romans and 1-2 Corinthians* (translated and edited by Gerald Bray; Downers Grove: IVP, 2009), 120 (PL 17:195).

5   Origen (185-254) was a biblical scholar from Alexandria, Egypt. See e.g. his commentary on Romans, Book 3 in Origen, *Commentary on the Epistle to the Romans, Books 1-5* (translated by Thomas Scheck; Washington: Catholic University of America, 2001), 178ff (PG 14:952-953).

6   See e.g. Chrysostom's Homily 7 on Romans 3:27 (PG 60:446 §4; NPNF 11:379); cf. Homily 8 on Romans 4:1 (PG 60:453; NPNF 11:385).

7   Cyprian (c.200-258) was Bishop of Carthage in what is now Tunisia. See e.g. his *Testimonies against the Jews*, Book 3, Section 42 (PL 4:725, 757-758; ANF 5:529, 545). Cf. his *Epistle to Cæcilius, on the Sacrament of the Cup of the Lord* (Epistola LXIII in PL 4:375-377 §4; Epistle LXII in ANF 5:359).

St Augustine,[8] Prosper,[9] Oecumenius,[10] Phocius,[11] Bernardus,[12] Anselm,[13] and many other Authors, Greek, and Latin.[14]

---

8 See e.g. Augustine's second exposition of Psalms 32 and 89 in E. B. Pusey (ed.), *Expositions on the Book of Psalms by S. Augustine* (Oxford, 1839), 1:284-285 4:264 (PL 36:261-262 §6; 37:1137 §7), and his book *On Faith and Works*, Chapter 14 (Section 21) in *Treatises on Marriage and Other Subjects* (edited by Roy Deferrari; Washington: Catholic University of America, 1969), 221ff (PL 40:211), and *On the Spirit and the Letter*, Chapters/Sections 11, 16, 45 (PL 44:206, 209-210, 228; NPNF 5:87, 89, 102).

9 Prosper (c.390-c.455) was a lay theologian from Aquitaine in France. See e.g. *The Call of All Nations,* Book 1, Chapter 17 (translated by P. De Letter; Westminster, M.D.: Newman Press, 1952), 60 (PL 51:669), as well as Epigram 8 (PL 51:501). Cf. *Letter to Rufinus,* §§ 7-10, and *On Grace and Free Will against Cassian* Chapter 10 §2 in Prosper of Aquitaine, *Defense of St Augustine* (translated by P. De Letter; New York: Newman Press, 1963), 27-29, 97 (PL 51:81-82, 240).

10 Oecumenius was from Thessaly in Greece, or perhaps somewhere in what is now Turkey, and wrote Bible commentaries sometime between the 6th-10th centuries. See his commentary on Romans 4:16 (PG 118: 401/2).

11 Photius (c.820-c.891) was Patriarch of Constantinople in what is now Turkey. He is quoted in the commentary on Romans 4:1 and 5:2 associated with Oecumenius, saying justification is "by faith alone" (PG 118:391/392, 407/8).

12 Bernard (1090-1153) was Abbot of Clairvaux in Burgundy, France. See e.g. his Sermons 22 §8 and 67 §10 on the Song of Songs, in *The Life and Works of Saint Bernard* (translated and edited by Samuel Eales; John Hodges: London, 1896), 4:128, 414 (PL 183:881, 1107), and *Tractatus de Baptismo*, Chapter 2 §8 in *Bernard of Clairvaux: On Baptism and the Office of Bishops* (translated by Pauline Matarasso; Liturgical Press, 2005) and PL 182:1036.

13 Anselm (1033-1109) was Archbishop of Canterbury. The most probable reference here, however, is to a commentary on Paul's epistles by Hervé of Déols (c.1080-1150)—a Benedictine Bible interpreter from the Abbey of Notre-Dame-du-Bourg-Dieu in Déols, Centre-Val de Loire, France—which was sometimes attributed to Anselm and circulated with his works. See e.g. on Romans 3:28, Romans 4:5, and 1 Corinthians 1:4 (PL 181:639-640, 645, 817).

14 To those noted above, we might add the standard Bible commentary of the later medieval and early modern period which says (on Romans 3:28) that "a person is made just *by faith alone* without preceding works". See *The Glossa Ordinaria on Romans* (trans. Michael Scott Woodward; Kalamazoo, Michigan: Medieval Institute Publications, 2011), 59 (PL 114:481). Cf. also the commentary of Peter Lombard (1099-1159) on Romans 3:28 (PL 191:1364-1365), and even *Pelagius's Commentary on St Paul's Epistle to the Romans* (translated by Theodore de Bruyn; Oxford: Clarendon Press, 1993), 63, 83, 85, 89, 112, 122 from the Latin in Alexander Souter, *Pelagius's Exposition of Thirteen Epistles of St Paul* (Volume 2; Cambridge: Cambridge University Press, 1926), 12, 34, 36, 41, 68, 81 from the first decade of the 5th century.

Nevertheless, this sentence, that we are justified by faith alone, is not meant by them in the sense that justifying faith is alone in a person, without true repentance, hope, charity, dread, and the fear of God, at any time and season. Nor when they say that we are justified freely do they mean that we should or might afterwards be idle, and that nothing should be required on our part afterwards. Neither do they mean that being justified without good works we should therefore do no good works at all, which we shall discuss further later. But this proposition, that we are justified only by faith, freely and without works, is spoken to take away clearly all thoughts of our works having merit, since they are unable to deserve our justification at God's hands. It most plainly expresses our weakness and the goodness of God, the great infirmity of ourselves and the might and power of God, the imperfection of our own works and the most abundant grace of our Saviour Christ. It therefore wholly ascribes the merit and deserving of our justification to Christ alone, and his most precious blood shedding.

This faith the holy scripture teaches us. This is the strong rock and foundation of Christian religion. All the old and ancient authors of Christ's church do approve this doctrine. This doctrine advances and sets forth the true glory of Christ, and beats down the vainglory of mankind. Whoever denies this is not be counted a true Christian, nor as one who sets forth Christ's glory, but as an adversary to Christ and his gospel, and one who advances the vainglory of mankind.

Misunderstandings of this doctrine

So this doctrine is most true, that we are justified freely without any merit of our own good works (as St Paul expresses it), and freely by this lively and perfect faith in Christ only (as the ancient authors used to put it). Yet this true doctrine must also be truly understood and most plainly declared, in case carnal people should make of it an excuse to live carnally, following the appetite and will of the world, the flesh, and the devil. And because no-one should be mistaken by misunderstanding this doctrine, I shall plainly and briefly declare the right understanding of it, so that no one can justly think it is an excuse for carnal liberty, to follow the desires of the flesh, or that it encourages any kind of sin to be committed, or any ungodly living to be indulged.

First, you must understand, that in our justification by Christ, our responsibility and God's responsibility are not the same. Justification is not our responsibility but God's, for we cannot make ourselves righteous by our own works, neither in part nor in whole. For that would be the greatest arrogance and presumption that Antichrist could set up against God, to affirm that someone might, by their own works, take away and purge their own sins, and so justify themselves. But justification is the responsibility of God alone, and is not a thing which we render to him, but which we receive from him. It is not something we give to him, but which we take from him, by his free mercy, and only by the merits of his most dearly beloved Son, our only Redeemer, Saviour, and Justifier—Jesus Christ.

So the true understanding of this doctrine—that we are justified freely by faith without works, or that we are justified by faith in Christ alone—is not that our own act (to believe in Christ) or that our faith in Christ (which is within us) is what justifies us and earns our justification for us. For that would be to count ourselves justified by some act or virtue that is within ourselves. But the true understanding and meaning of it is that although we hear God's word, and believe it, although we have faith, hope, charity, repentance, dread, and fear of God within us, and do however many good works—yet, we must renounce the merit of all our said virtues, of faith, hope, charity, and all other virtues and good deeds, which we either have done, shall do, or can do, as things that are far too weak and insufficient, and imperfect, to deserve cancellation of our sins and our justification.

Therefore, we must trust only in God's mercy, and that sacrifice which our High Priest and Saviour, Christ Jesus the Son of God, once offered for us upon the cross. By this we obtain God's grace, and the forgiveness both of our original sin in baptism as well as all actual sin committed by us after our baptism—if we truly repent, and turn sincerely to him again.[15] In this matter of forgiveness for sin, St John the Baptist (although he was a very virtuous and godly man) pointed the people away from himself, and pointed them to Christ, saying "Behold, the Lamb of God, who takes away the sins of the world!" (John 1:29). In the same way, as great and as godly a virtue as living faith is, yet it points us away from itself, and sends or points us to Christ, that only by him may we have cancellation of our sins, or justification. So that our faith in Christ says to us (as it were) thus: "It is not I that take away your sins, but it is Christ only, and to him alone I send you for that purpose, renouncing all your good virtues, words, thoughts, and works, and only putting your trust in Christ."

A Trusting and Obedient Heart

It has been manifestly declared to you, that no one can fulfil the Law of God, and therefore by the Law all are condemned. It therefore follows necessarily that some other thing should be required for our salvation than the Law: and that is, a true and a living faith in Christ, bringing forth good works, and a life according to God's commandments. And you have also heard the ancient authors' opinion of this saying, "Faith in Christ alone justifies a person", so plainly declared. So you see that the very true meaning of this proposition or saying, "We are justified only by faith in Christ" (according to the meaning of the old ancient authors) is this: We put our faith in Christ, that we are justified by him alone, that we are justified by God's free mercy, and the merits of our Saviour Christ alone. By no virtue or good works of our own that are in

---

15 See Article 31 which says that "The Offering of Christ once made is that perfect redemption, propitiation, and satisfaction, for all the sins of the whole world, both original and actual; and there is none other satisfaction for sin, but that alone."

us, or that we are able to have or to do, can we deserve the same. Christ himself is the only meritorious cause of our justification.

CLARITY AMIDST CONTENTION

Here you perceive many words are used, to avoid contention in words with those who delight to brawl about words; and also to show the true meaning, to avoid evil talking and misunderstanding. And yet, it is possible that all of this will not satisfy those who are contentious. Such people will always invent things to contend about, even when they have no reason to do so. We are more concerned with those who are most desirous to know the truth and to profit by it, than we are with those who (when it is plain enough) want to contend about it, and with contentious and critical complaining to obscure and darken it.

It is true that our own works do not justify us, to speak properly of our justification; that is to say, our works do not merit or deserve cancellation of our sins, and make we who are unrighteous, righteous before God. But God, of his own mercy, justifies us only through the merits of his Son Jesus Christ—not because we deserve it, but because he does. Nevertheless, faith directly sends us to Christ for cancellation of our sins (and that by faith given to us by God), so that we embrace the promise of God's mercy, and of the forgiveness of our sins. None of our other virtues or works can properly do this; therefore scripture says that faith without works justifies.

Since it is the same thing, in effect, to say "faith without works" and "only faith justifies us", the old ancient fathers of the church from time to time spoke of our justification in this way: "only faith justifies us", meaning nothing else than what St Paul meant when he said faith without works justifies us (Romans 3:28). And because all this is brought to pass only through the merit and worthiness of our Saviour Christ, and not through our merits, or through the merit of any virtue that we have within us, or of any work that comes from us: therefore in respect of merit and deserving we forsake faith, works, and all other virtues. For our own imperfection is so great, through the corruption of original sin, that everything within us is imperfect—faith, charity, hope, dread, thoughts, words, and works—and therefore not able to merit or deserve any part of our justification for us. And we speak in this way, humbling ourselves to God, to give all the glory to our Saviour Christ, who is best worthy to have it.

You have heard about the role of God in our justification, and how we receive it from him freely, by his mercy, without deserving it, through true and lively faith. Now you shall hear the role and duty of a Christian to God, what we ought on our part to render back to God for his great mercy and goodness.

THE DUTY OF A JUSTIFIED CHRISTIAN

Our role is not to pass the time of this present life unfruitfully and idly after we are baptised or justified, not caring how few good works we do to the glory of God and the profit of our neighbours. Much less is it our role, after we are once made Christ's members, to live contrary to him, making ourselves members of the devil, walking after his enticements and after the suggestions of the world and the flesh, by which we know that we serve the world and the devil, and not God. For that faith which brings forth (without repentance) either evil works or no good works, is not a right, pure, and living faith, but a dead, devilish, counterfeit, and insincere faith, as St Paul and St James call it (2 Timothy 3:5, Titus 1:16, James 2:17-26).

For even the devils know and believe that Christ was born of a virgin, that he fasted forty days and forty nights without meat and drink, that he worked all kinds of miracles, showing himself to be truly God. They believe also that Christ, for our sakes, suffered a most painful death, to redeem us from eternal death, and that he rose again from death on the third day. They believe that he ascended into heaven, and that he sits on the right hand of the Father, and at the last end of this world he shall come again and judge both the living and the dead. These articles of our faith the devils believe, and so they believe all things that are written in the New and Old Testament to be true. And yet, for all this faith, they are but devils, remaining still in their damnable state, lacking the very true Christian faith.

For the right and true Christian faith is not only to believe that holy scripture and all these articles of our faith are true, but also to have a sure trust and confidence in God's merciful promises, to be saved from everlasting damnation by Christ. From this follows a loving heart to obey his commandments. No devil has this true Christian faith, nor does any person who in the outward profession of their mouth and in their outward receiving of the sacraments, in coming to Church and in all other outward appearances, seems to be a Christian, and yet in their life and works shows the contrary. For how can someone have this true faith, this sure trust and confidence in God, that by the merits of Christ their sins are forgiven, and be reconciled to the favour of God, and be partaker of the kingdom of heaven by Christ, when they live an ungodly life and deny Christ in their deeds?

Surely no such ungodly person can have this faith and trust in God. For as they know Christ to be the only saviour of the world, so they know also that the wicked shall not possess the kingdom of God (1 Corinthians 6:9, Galatians 5:19-21, Ephesians 5:5). They know that God hates unrighteousness, that he will destroy all those that speak untruly (Psalm 5:5-6), that those who have done good works (which cannot be done without a lively faith in Christ) shall come forth into the resurrection of life, and those that have done evil shall come to the resurrection of judgment (John 5:29). They also know very well that to those who are contentious, and to those who will not be obedient to the truth but will obey unrighteousness, shall come indignation, wrath, and affliction, and so forth (Romans 2:8-9).

CONSIDER ALL HIS BENEFITS!

Therefore, to conclude: let us consider the infinite benefits of God, shown and given to us mercifully although we do not deserve them. Let us consider that God has not only created us out of nothing, and from a piece of vile clay, but of his infinite goodness has exalted us (as touching our soul) to his own image and likeness. We were condemned to hell, and death eternal, but he has given his own natural Son (who is God eternal, immortal, and equal to himself in power and glory) to be incarnated, and to take our mortal nature upon him, with the infirmities of it, and in the same nature to suffer most shameful and painful death for our offences. He did this to justify us, and to restore us to life everlasting, so making us also his dear children, brethren to his only Son our Saviour Christ (Hebrews 2:11), and inheritors forever with him of his eternal kingdom of heaven.

These great and merciful benefits of God (if they are well considered) neither give us an excuse to be idle and to live without doing any good works, nor yet stir us up by any means to do evil things. On the contrary, if we are not desperate persons, and our hearts harder than stones, they move us to give ourselves wholly to God with all our will, hearts, might, and power, to serve him in all good deeds, obeying his commandments during our lives, to seek in all things his glory and honour not our sensual pleasures and vainglory, evermore dreading willingly to offend such a merciful God and loving redeemer, in word, thought, or deed. And these benefits of God deeply considered, move us for his sake also to be ever ready to give ourselves to our neighbours and, as much as lies in us, to study with all our endeavour to do good to everyone. These are the fruits of true faith, to do good as much as lies in us to everyone, and above all things and in all things to advance the glory of God, from whom alone we have our sanctification, justification, salvation, and redemption (1 Corinthians 1:30)—to whom be glory, praise, and honour forever, world without end. *Amen.*

TRUE AND LIVING CHRISTIAN FAITH

O ur first approach to God (good Christian people) is through faith, through which (as it was declared in the last sermon) we are justified before God. And in case anyone should be deceived, for lack of a right understanding of this, it is diligently to be noted that faith is taken in the scripture in two ways.

TWO KINDS OF FAITH

There is one kind of faith, which in scripture is called a dead faith. This brings forth no good works, but is idle, barren, and unfruit-ful. And this faith, by the holy apostle St James, is compared to the faith of devils, who believe God to be true and just, and tremble for fear, yet they do nothing well, but all evil (James 2:17-18). This is the kind of faith which wicked and disobedient Christian people have who "confess God" (as St Paul says) with their mouth, "but deny him in their deeds, being detestable, and without the right faith, and unfit for any good work" (Titus 1:16). And this faith is a persuasion and belief in someone's heart, by which they know that there is a God, and assent to all the truth of God's most holy word contained in the holy scripture. But it consists only in believing that the word of God is true.

---

* The original title of this Homily was *A Short Declaration of True and Living Christian Faith*

This is not properly called faith. If one were to read Caesar's *Commentaries*, believing them to be true, one would have through this a knowledge of Caesar's life and noble acts, because you believe the history of Caesar.[1] Yet it is not properly said that such a person "believes in Caesar", since they do not look to him for any help or benefit. Even so, a person may believe that everything that is spoken about God in the Bible is true, and yet live such an ungodly life that they cannot hope to enjoy the promises and benefits of God. Although it may be said that such a person has a faith and belief in the words of God, yet it is not properly said that they believe in God. They do not have such a faith and trust in God that they may surely look for grace, mercy, and eternal life from God's hand, but rather for indignation and punishment, according to the merits of their wicked life. For as it is written in a book said to be by Didymus of Alexandria, "in that faith without works is dead, it is not now faith, just as a dead man is not a man."[2] This dead faith therefore is not the sure and substantial faith which saves sinners.

There is another kind of faith spoken of in scripture, which is not (like the previous sort of faith) idle, unfruitful, and dead, but works through love, as St Paul declares (Galatians 5:6). As the other, vain faith is called a dead faith, so may this be called a living or lively faith. And this is not only the common belief in the articles of our faith,[3] but it is also a sure trust and confidence in the mercy of God through our Lord Jesus Christ, and a steadfast hope of all good things to be received from God's hand. And although we, through infirmity or temptation from our spiritual enemy, fall

---

1   This refers to the histories of the Gallic War and Roman Civil War written by Julius Caesar (100-44 BC) in the first century BC: *Commentarii de Bello Civili* and *Commentarii de Bello Gallico* (LCL 39 and 72).

2   Didymus of Alexandria (313-398), also known as Didymus the Blind, was a theologian from Alexandria, Egypt. The reference is to his brief commentary on James 2:26 (PG 39:1752), though there remain some doubts as to the authorship of this work.

3   This refers to the articles of the Creed, rather than the *Thirty-nine Articles of Religion*.

from him by sin, yet if we return again to him by true repentance, he will forgive and forget our offences for his Son our Saviour Jesus Christ's sake, and will make us inheritors with him of his everlasting kingdom. And in the meantime, until that kingdom comes, he will be our protector and defender in all perils and dangers, whatever happens. And though he may sometimes send us sharp adversity, yet he will evermore be a loving Father to us, correcting us for our sin, but not finally withdrawing his mercy from us if we trust in him and commit ourselves wholly to him, hang only upon him, and call upon him, ready to obey and serve him.

This is true, living, and sincere Christian faith, and is not in the mouth and outward profession only, but it lives and stirs inwardly, in the heart. And this faith is not without hope and trust in God, nor without the love of God and of our neighbours, nor without the fear of God, nor without the desire to hear God's word, and to follow it in renouncing evil, and gladly doing all good works.

This faith (as St Paul describes it) is the sure ground and foundation of the benefits which we ought to look for and trust to receive from God, the assurance and sure expectation of them, although they do not yet appear to our senses (Hebrews 11:1). And afterwards he says, "The one who comes to God must believe both that he exists, and that he is a merciful rewarder of those who seek him" (Hebrews 11:6). And nothing commends good people to God so much as this assured faith and trust in him.

THE FRUITFULNESS OF TRUE FAITH

Of this faith, three things are specially to be noted. First, that this faith does not lie dead in the heart, but is lively and fruitful in bringing forth good works. Second, that without it, no good works that are acceptable and pleasing to God can be done. Third, what manner of good works they are, that this faith brings forth.

For the first, just as light cannot be hidden, but will show itself at one place or other, so a true faith cannot be kept secret. When occasion is offered, it will break out, and show itself by good works. The living body of a person will always be busy doing what natural and living bodies do to nourish and preserve themselves, as they have need, opportunity, and occasion. In the same way, the soul that has a lively faith in it will not be unoccupied, but will always be doing some good work, which will show that it is alive. Therefore when people hear in the scriptures such high commendations of faith—that it makes us please God, to live with God, and to be the children of God—if they then fantasise that they are set at liberty from doing all good works, and may live as they lust, they trifle with God and deceive themselves. And it is a manifest token that they are far from having a true and living faith, and also far from knowledge of what true faith means.

For the very sure and living Christian faith is not only to believe everything about God which is contained in holy scripture. It is also an earnest trust and confidence in God, that he regards us and that he is careful over us, as the father is over the child whom he loves. It is confidence that he will be merciful to us for his only Son's sake, and that we have our Saviour Christ as our perpetual advocate and Priest, in whose merits, sacrificial offering, and suffering alone we trust that our offences are continually washed and purged, whenever we (repenting truly) return to him with our whole heart, steadfastly determining with ourselves, through his grace, to obey and serve him in keeping his commandments, and never to turn back again to sin. Such is true faith, that the scripture commends so much.

When such faith sees and considers what God has done for us, it is moved through the continual assistance of the Spirit of God to serve and please him, to keep his favour, to fear his displeasure, to continue his obedient children, showing thankfulness in return to him by observing or keeping his commandments, and that freely, chiefly for true love and not for dread of punishment or love of temporal reward, considering how clearly, and undeservedly we have received his mercy and pardon freely.

This true faith will show itself, and cannot long be idle. For as it is written, "The righteous will live by their faith" (Habakkuk 2:4; Romans 1:17). It never sleeps nor is idle, when it should be awake and well occupied. And God, by his Prophet Jeremiah, says that "blessed is the one who trusts in the LORD, whose confidence is in him. They are like a tree planted by water, that sends out its roots to the stream. It does not fear when the heat comes; for its leaves are always green. It has no anxiety in the year of drought and never fails to bear fruit." (Jeremiah 17:7-8). Even so, faithful people (putting away all fear of adversity) will show forth the fruit of their good works, as occasion is offered to do them.

FAITH AND WORKS

You have heard in the first part of this sermon, that there are two kinds of faith, a dead and unfruitful faith, and a lively faith that expresses itself through love (Galatians 5:6). The first is unprofitable, whereas the second is necessary for the obtaining of our salvation. This true faith has charity always joined to it, and is fruitful, and brings forth all good works. Now, let us hear further on this same subject.

The wise man says, "The one who believes in God will listen to his commandments."[4] For if we do not show ourselves faithful in our lives, the faith which we pretend to have is but a false faith: because the true Christian faith is manifestly shown by good living, and not by words only, as St Augustine says, "Good living cannot be separated from true faith, which works by love."[5] And St Chrysostom says, "Faith of itself is full of good works: as soon as someone believes, they shall be garnished with them."[6]

---

4 From the apocryphal book of Ecclesiasticus or The Wisdom of Jesus the Son of Sirach, 32:24.

5 See his comment on John 5:28-29 in *On Faith and Works*, Chapter 23, Section 42 in *Treatises on Marriage and Other Subjects* (edited by Roy Deferrari; Washington: Catholic University of America, 1969), 221ff (PL 40:224).

6 The author of the work from which this comes—*De Fide et Lege Naturae*—is unknown, but since their works long circulated alongside Chrysostom's, they are known as Pseudo-Chrysostom. See PG 48:1081 for this comment on John 6:28-29.

FAITH AGAINST THE WORLD

How plentiful this faith is of good works, and how it makes the work of one person more acceptable to God than those of another, St Paul teaches at large in Hebrews 11. He says that faith made the offering of Abel better than the offering of Cain (Hebrews 11:4; Genesis 4:3-5). It made Noah build the Ark (Hebrews 11:7; Genesis 6:22). It made Abraham forsake his country, and all his friends, and to go into a far country, there to dwell among strangers (Hebrews 11:8-10; Genesis 11:31, 12:1-5). So also did Isaac and Jacob, solely depending only on the help and trust that they had in God. And when they came to the country which God promised them, they built no cities, towns, or houses, but lived like strangers in tents, that might every day be moved (Hebrews 11:9; Genesis 13, 18). Their trust was so much in God, that they did not trust in any worldly thing, because God had prepared for them better dwelling places in heaven of his own foundation and building.

This faith made Abraham ready at God's commandment, to offer his own son and heir Isaac, whom he loved so much, and by whom he was promised to have innumerable offspring, among whom one would be born in whom all nations would be blessed. He trusted so much in God, that even if he was slain, he knew that God was able by his omnipotent power to raise him from death, and perform his promise (Hebrews 11:17-19; Genesis 22). He did not distrust the promise of God, although everything seemed contrary to his reason. He truly believed that God would not forsake him in death and in the famine that was in the land. And in all other dangers that he was brought to, he always trusted that God should be his God, and his protector, whatever he saw to the contrary.

This faith worked in the heart of Moses, so that he refused to be known as the son of Pharoah's daughter, and to have great inheritance in Egypt, thinking it better to have affliction and sorrow with the people of God, than to live pleasantly in sin for a time

with evil people (Hebrews 11:25; Exodus 2). By faith he cared not
for the threatening of King Pharaoh: for his trust was so in God,
that he did not live for happiness in this world, but looked for the
reward to come in heaven, setting his heart on the invisible God,
as if he had seen him ever present before his eyes (Hebrews 11:27).
By faith, the children of Israel passed through the Red Sea (Hebrews 11:29; Exodus 14). By faith, the walls of Jericho fell down
without a stroke (Hebrews 11:30; Joshua 6:20), and many other
wonderful miracles have been done. In all good people who have
lived before us, faith has brought forth their good works, and obtained the promises of God. Faith has stopped the lions' mouths
(Hebrews 11:33; Daniel 6:16-23). Faith has quenched the force
of fire (Hebrews 11:34; Daniel 3:13-28). Faith has escaped the
edge of the sword. Faith has given strength to the weak, victory in
battle, overthrown the armies of infidels, raised the dead to life.
Faith has made good people endure adversity well, as some have
been mocked and whipped, bound, and cast in prison; some have
lost all their goods and lived in great poverty; some have wandered
in mountains, hills, and wilderness; some have been racked, some
slain, some stoned, some sawn, some cut in pieces, some beheaded,
some burnt without mercy, and asked not to be delivered, because
they looked to rise again to a better state.

One Christ, One Spirit
All these Fathers, Martyrs, and other holy people whom St Paul
spoke of had their faith surely fixed on God, when all the world
was against them. They did not only know God to be the Lord,
maker, and governor of all people in the world, but they also had
a special confidence and trust that he was and would be their God,
their comforter, aid, helper, maintainer, and defender. This is the
Christian faith which these holy people had, and we also ought
to have. And although they were not named Christians, yet was it
a Christian faith that they had, for they looked for all benefits of
God the Father, through the merits of his Son Jesus Christ, as we

now do. The difference between them and us is that they looked forward to when Christ would come, and we are in the time when he has come. Therefore, says St Augustine, "The time is altered and changed, but not the faith. For we both have one faith in one Christ."[7]

The same Holy Spirit that we have, they also had, says St Paul (2 Corinthians 4:13). For as the Holy Spirit teaches us to trust in God, and to call upon him as our Father, he also taught them to say, as it is written, "You, LORD, are our Father and Redeemer, and your name is without beginning and everlasting" (Isaiah 63:16). God gave them grace to be his children, as he does to us now. But now by the coming of our Saviour Christ, we have received the Spirit of God in our hearts more abundantly, by whom we may conceive a greater faith, and a surer trust than many of them had. But, in effect, they and we are all one: we have the same faith that they had in God, and they the same that we have. And St Paul so much extols their faith, because we should give ourselves wholly to Christ, both in profession and living, now that Christ has come, no less than the old fathers did before his coming, but rather more. And from all that St Paul says, it is evident that the true, living, Christian faith, is no dead, vain, or unfruitful thing, but a thing of perfect virtue, of wonderful operation or working, and strength, bringing forth all good motions, and good works.

TRUE FAITH WORKS

All holy scripture agrees and bears witness that a true, lively faith in Christ brings forth good works. And therefore everyone must examine and test themselves diligently, to know whether they have the same true, lively faith in their heart sincerely, or not—which they shall know by the fruits of it. Many who have professed the faith of Christ have made this error: that they thought they knew God, and believed in him, when in their life they declared the contrary. St

---

7   See Augustine, *In Ioannis Evangelium Tractatus*, Tract 45, Section 9 on John 10:1-10 (PL 35:1722; NPNF 7:252).

John confutes this error in his first epistle, writing that "We know we have come to know him, if we keep his commandments. Anyone who says, 'I know him,' but does not do what he commands, is a liar, and the truth is not in them" (1 John 2:3-4). And again he says, "No one who lives in him keeps sinning. No one who continues to sin has either seen him or known him. Children, do not let anyone deceive you" (1 John 3:6-7). Moreover, he also says, "This is how we know that we belong to the truth and how we reassure our hearts in his presence: If our hearts condemn us, we know that God is greater than our hearts, and he knows everything. Beloved, if our hearts do not condemn us, we have confidence before God and receive from him whatever we ask, because we keep his commandments and do what pleases him" (1 John 3:19-22).

And yet further he says "Everyone who believes that Jesus is the Christ is born from God," and, "We know that anyone born from God does not keep sinning. The One who was born of God protects them, and the evil one cannot touch them" (1 John 5:1, 18). And finally, he concludes and reveals why he wrote this epistle, saying, "For this reason I have written to you, who believe in the name of the Son of God, so that you may know that you have eternal life" (1 John 5:13). And in his third epistle, John confirms the whole matter of faith and works in a few words, saying "Whoever does what is good is from God. Anyone who does what is evil has not seen God." (3 John 11). St John says that the lively knowledge and faith of God brings forth good works and, in the same way, he says that hope and charity cannot stand with evil living. Of hope, he writes thus: "we know that when Christ appears, we shall be like him, for we will see him as he is. Everyone who has this hope in him purifies themselves, just as he is pure" (1 John 3:2-3). And of charity he says these words, "if anyone keeps his word, love for God is truly made complete in them" (1 John 2:5). And again he says, "this is love for God: keeping his commands" (1 John 5:3).

St John wrote this, not as a subtle saying, a fantasy of his own devising, but as a most certain and necessary truth, taught to him by Christ himself, the eternal and infallible Truth, who in many places most clearly affirms that faith, hope, and charity cannot consist or stand without good and godly works. Of faith, he says "Whoever believes in the Son has eternal life, but whoever rejects the Son will not see life, for God's wrath remains on them" (John 3:36). And the same he confirms with a double oath, saying, "Truly truly I say to you, the one who believes has eternal life" (John 6:47). Now, since the one who believes in Christ has everlasting life, it must consequently follow that the one who has this faith must also have good works, and be studious to observe God's commandments obediently. For to those who have evil works, and lead their life in disobedience, and transgression or breaking of God's commandments, without repentance, belongs not everlasting life but everlasting death, as Christ himself says "those who do well shall go into eternal life but those who do evil shall go into the everlasting fire" (Matthew 25:46; John 5:29). And again he says,

"It is done! I am the Alpha and the Omega, the beginning and the end. To those who are thirsty I will give water from the spring of the water of life, as a gift. The one who is victorious will inherit all this, and I will be their God and they will be my children. But as for the cowardly, the unbelieving, the vile, the murderers, the sexually immoral, those who practice magic arts, the idolaters and all liars—they will be given the fiery lake of burning sulphur. This is the second death." (Revelation 21:6-8)

Christ undoubtedly affirms that true faith brings forth good works. And in the same way, he says of love that "Whoever has my commands and keeps them is the one who loves me" (John 14:21), adding "Anyone who loves me will obey my teaching... Anyone who does not love me will not obey my teaching" (John 14:23-24). And as the love of God is proven by good works, so also is the fear of God, as the wise man says, "The fear of God puts away sin", and "The one who fears God will do good works".[8]

---

8   Quotations from the apocryphal book of Sirach 1:21, 15:1.

THE PROOF OF FAITH

You have heard in the second part of this sermon, that no one should think that they have that lively faith which scripture commands when they do not live obediently to God's laws, for all good works spring out of that faith. And it has also been declared to you by examples that faith makes people steadfast, quiet, and patient in all affliction. Now, let us hear further on this same subject.

DO NOT DECEIVE YOURSELF

Some may soon deceive themselves and think in their own imagination that by faith they know God, love him, fear him, and belong to him, when in actual fact they do no such thing. For the proof of all these things is a truly godly and Christian life. The one who feels their heart set to seek God's honour, and studies to know the will and commandments of God, and to frame their lives accordingly, and does not lead their life in pursuit of the desire of their own flesh, to serve the devil by sin, but sets their mind to serve God for his own sake, and for his sake also to love all their neighbours, whether they are friends or adversaries, doing good to everyone (as opportunity serves) and willingly hurting no one: such a person may well rejoice in God, perceiving by the course of their life that they sincerely have the right knowledge of God, a lively faith, a steadfast hope, a true and unfeigned love, and fear of God.

But those who cast away the yoke of God's commandments from their neck, and give themselves to live without true repentance, pursuing their own sensual mind and pleasure, not caring to know God's word, and much less to live according to it: such a person clearly deceives themselves, and does not see their own heart if they think that they either know God, love him, fear him, or trust in him.

Some perhaps imagine in themselves that they belong to God, even though they live in sin, and so they come to church, and show themselves as God's dear children. But St John says plainly,

"If we say that we have any company with God, and yet walk in darkness, we lie" (1 John 1:6). Others vainly think that they know and love God, although they do not keep the commandments. But St John says clearly, "Whoever says, 'I know God,' but does not do what he commands is a liar" (1 John 2:4). Some falsely persuade themselves that they love God, when they hate their neighbours. But St John manifestly says, "Whoever claims to love God, and yet hates their brother or sister, is a liar," and, "Whoever claims to be in the light but hates their brother or sister is still in the darkness. Whoever loves their brother and sister lives in the light, and there is nothing in them to cause them to stumble. But whoever hates their brother or sister is in the darkness and walks in the darkness. They do not know where they are going, because the darkness has blinded their eyes" (1 John 4:20, 2:9-11). And, moreover, he says, "This is how we know who are the children of God and who are the children of the devil: Whoever does not do what is right is not God's child, nor is anyone who does not love their brother and sister" (1 John 3:10).

Do not deceive yourselves, therefore, thinking that you have faith in God, or that you love God, or trust in him, or fear him, when you live in sin. For then your ungodly and sinful life declares the contrary, whatever you may say or think. Christians should have this true Christian faith, and examine themselves whether they have it or not, and know what it is and how it works in them. We cannot trust the world. The world and all that is in it is but vanity. It is God who must be our defence and protection against all temptation of wickedness and sin, errors, superstition, idolatry, and all evil. If the whole world was on our side, and God against us, what could the world benefit us? Therefore, let us set our whole faith and trust in God, and neither the world, the devil, nor all the power of them shall prevail against us.

Let us therefore (good Christian people), test and examine our faith, and what it is. Let us not flatter ourselves, but look at our works, and so judge of our faith. Christ himself speaks of this matter, and says, "The tree is known by the fruit" (Matthew 12:33). Therefore let us do good works, and by this declare our faith to be a living Christian faith. Let us by such virtues as ought to spring out of faith, show our election to be sure and stable, as St Peter teaches: "make every effort to confirm your calling and election" (2 Peter 1:10). And he also says, "make every effort to add to your faith, goodness; and to goodness, add knowledge; and to knowledge, add self-control; and to self-control, add perseverance; and to perseverance, add godliness; and to godliness, add brotherly affection; and to brotherly affection, add love" (2 Peter 1:5-7). So we shall show indeed that we have a living Christian faith, and may both better assure our conscience that we are in the right faith, and also by these means confirm this to others. If these fruits do not follow, we only mock with God, deceiving ourselves and others. We may well bear the name of Christian, but we lack the true faith that belongs to it. For true faith always brings forth good works, as St James says: "Show me your faith by your deeds" (James 2:18).

COUNTERFEIT FAITH

Your deeds and works must be an open testimonial of your faith; otherwise, your faith (being without good works) is only the faith of devils, the faith of the wicked, a fantasy of faith, and not a true Christian faith. Devils and evil people are no better off for their counterfeit faith, but it is to them even more a cause of damnation. In the same way, those who are Christians and have received knowledge of God and of Christ's merits, and yet have a set purpose to live idly without good works, thinking the name of a naked faith to be sufficient for them—upon such presumptuous persons, and wilful sinners, the great vengeance of God must remain, and eternal punishment in hell, prepared for the unjust and the wicked. The same is true for those who set their minds upon the vain pleasures of this world, and live in sin without repentance, not bearing the fruits that belong to such a high profession.

Therefore as you profess the name of Christ (good Christian

people), let no such fantasy and imagination of faith at any time beguile you. But be sure of your faith; prove it by your living; look at the fruits that come from it; mark the increase of love and charity by it towards God and your neighbour; and so shall you perceive it to be a true and living faith. If you feel and perceive such a faith in you, rejoice in it; and be diligent to maintain it, and keep it still in you. Let it be daily increasing, more and more, by doing good, and so shall you be sure that you shall please God by this faith, and at the length (as other faithful people have done before) you shall (when God wills it) come to him, and receive the end and final reward of your faith (as St Peter calls it) "the salvation of your souls" (1 Peter 1:9). May God grant us this, which he has promised to his faithful, and to him be all honour and glory, world without end. *Amen.*

Faith and Good Works

Faith is needed to please God

In the last sermon it was declared to you what the lively and true faith of a Christian is—that it does not cause someone to be idle, but to be occupied in bringing forth good works, as occasion serves. Now by God's grace we shall declare the second thing to be noted about faith—that without it, no good work can be done that is accepted and pleasant to God. For our Saviour Christ says, "As the branch cannot bear fruit by itself, unless it abides in the vine, neither can you, unless you abide in me. I am the vine; you are the branches. Whoever abides in me and I in them, they are the ones who bear much fruit, for apart from me you can do nothing" (John 15:4-5). And St Paul proves that Enoch had faith because he pleased God, for without faith (he says), "it is not possible to please God" (Hebrews 11:5-6). And again to the Romans he says that "whatever work is done without faith, it is sin" (Romans 14:23).

Faith gives life to the soul. Those who lack faith are dead to God just as those whose bodies lack souls are dead to the world. Without faith, everything we do is dead in God's eyes, however great and glorious it may seem to other people. In the same way as an engraving or a painting is only a dead representation of a thing itself, and is without life or any sort of movement, so also in God's eyes are the works of all those who do not have faith. They appear

---

* The original title of this Homily was *A Homily of Good Works Annexed to Faith*.

to be lively works, but they are in fact dead and do not lead to everlasting life. They are but shadows and shows of lively and good things, and not good and living things in reality. For true faith gives life to the works, and out of such faith comes good works that are very good works indeed. But without faith, no work is good before God.

THE ONE THING NECESSARY

As St Augustine says: "We must set no good works before faith, nor think that before faith a person may do any good works: for such works, although they seem to people to be praiseworthy, yet they are in fact only vain," and not allowed before God. "They are like the course of a horse that runs out of the track, which makes a great effort, but to no purpose. Let no one therefore," says he, "reckon on their good works before their faith. Where faith is not, good works are not. The intent," he says, "makes the good works, but faith must guide and order the intent of person."[1] And Christ says, "If your eye is bad, your whole body is full of darkness" (Matthew 6:23). "The eye signifies the intent," says St Augustine, "with which someone does a thing."[2] So that the one who does not do their good works with a godly intent, and a true faith that works by love, their whole body, that is to say the whole number of their works, is dark, and there is no light in them.

For good deeds are not measured by the facts themselves, and so distinguished from vices, but by the ends and intents for which they were done.[3] An unbelieving person could clothe the na-

1   See Augustine's second exposition of Psalm 32:1 in Pusey (ed.), *Expositions on the Book of Psalms by S. Augustine*, 1:281 (PL 36:259-260 §4). Cf. *The Glossa Ordinaria on Romans*, 211 (on Romans 14:23; PL 114:516), and Lombard, *Sentences*, 2.40.1.2 in Giulio Silano, *The Sentences: Book 2 On Creation* (Toronto: Pontifical Institute of Mediaeval Studies, 2008), 198 (PL 192:747).

2   Augustine, *Contra Iulianum* 4.3.33 in *Saint Augustine Against Julian* (trans. Matthew Schumacher; New York: Fathers of the Church Inc., 1957), 197 (PL 44:755). Cf. Augustine, *De Sermone Domini in Monte*, 2.13.45 (PL 34:1289; NPNF 5:48).

3   Augustine, *Contra Iulianum* 4.3.21 in *Saint Augustine Against Julian*, 186 (PL

ked, feed the hungry, and do other such works, yet because they do not do them in faith, for the honour and love of God, they are but dead, vain, and fruitless works to him.[4] It is faith which commends the work to God: for (as St Augustine says), "whether you will or not, 'that work which does not come from faith, is nothing.'"[5] Where faith in Christ is not the foundation, there is no good work, whatever building we make.

There is one work, in which are all good works—that is, faith, which expresses itself by love.[6] If you have it, you have the ground of all good works. For the virtues of strength, wisdom, temperance, and justice are all referred to this same faith.[7] Without this faith we do not have them, but only the names and shadows of them, as St Augustine said: "All the life of those who lack true faith is sin, and nothing is good, without him who is the author of goodness. Where he is not, there is only false virtue, even in the best works."[8] And St Augustine, expounding this verse of the Psalm—"The swallow has found a nest where she may keep her young birds" (Psalm 84:3)—says that Jews, heretics, and pagans do good works (they clothe the naked, feed the poor, and do other good works of mercy), but because they are not done in the true faith, the birds are lost. But if they remain in faith, then faith is the nest and safeguard of their birds, that is to say, the safeguard of their good works, that the reward of them is not utterly lost.[9]

44:749).

4   Augustine, *Contra Iulianum* 4.3.30-33 in *Saint Augustine Against Julian*, 194-197 (PL 44:753-754).

5   Augustine, *Contra Iulianum* 4.3.32 in *Saint Augustine Against Julian*, 196 (PL 44:755), alluding to Romans 14:23.

6   See Augustine's exposition of Psalm 90:17 in Pusey (ed.), *Expositions on the Book of Psalms by S. Augustine*, 4:281 (PL 37:1149), alluding to Galatians 5:6.

7   Augustine, *Contra Iulianum* 4.3.19 in *Saint Augustine Against Julian*, 184 (PL 44:747).

8   T his saying of Augustine is recorded in Prosper of Aquitaine, *Liber Sententiarum ex Operibus S. Augustini Delibatarum*, §106 (PL 51:441).

9   See Augustine's exposition of Psalm 84:3 in Pusey (ed.), *Expositions on the Book of Psalms by S. Augustine*, 4:153 (PL 37:1060-1061 §7).

And this matter (which St Augustine disputes about at length in many books), St Ambrose concludes in a few words saying, "The one who would withstand vice by nature, either by natural will or reason, garnishes the time of this life in vain and does not attain the very true virtues. For without the worshipping of the true God, that which seems to be virtue, is vice."[10]

FAITH ALONE SAVES

And yet most plainly to this purpose, St John Chrysostom writes in this way: "You shall find many which have not the true faith, and are not of the flock of Christ, and yet (it appears) they flourish in good works of mercy. You shall find them full of pity, compassion, and given to justice, and yet for all that they have no fruit of their works, because the chief work is lacking. For when the Jews asked of Christ what they should do to do good works, he answered 'This is the work of God, to believe in him whom he sent' (John 6:28-29). He called faith the work of God. And as soon as someone has faith, they shall flourish in good works, for faith of itself is full of good works, and nothing is good without faith."[11] And he says, by way of a comparison, that "those who glisten and shine in good works, without faith in God, are like dead people, who have large and precious tombs, and yet it does not benefit them at all." He continues:

> "Faith should not be naked, without good works, for then it would not be true faith. And when it is joined to works, it is yet above the works. For as people first have life, and after that are nourished: so must our faith in Christ go before, and afterwards be nourished with good works. Life may be without nourishment, but nourish-

---

10 This is more usually identified now as a work of Prosper of Aquitaine, rather than of Ambrose (see PL 17:1067). Prosper of Aquitaine, *The Call of All Nations*, 7, 34 (Book 1, Chapter 7; PL 51:653).

11 The author of the work from which this comes—*De Fide et Lege Naturae*—is unknown, but since their works long circulated alongside Chrysostom's they are known as Pseudo-Chrysostom. See PG 48:1081-1082 for the Greek and Latin on which the Homily's translation in this paragraph and the next is based.

ment cannot be without life. A person needs to be nourished by good works, but first they must have faith. The one who does good deeds, yet without faith, has no life. I can show a man who lived and came to heaven by faith without works; but without faith, no one ever had life. The thief who was hanged, when Christ suffered, did believe only, and the most merciful God justified him (Luke 23:40-43). It is true, and I will not contend about it, that he lacked time to do good works, or else he would have done them. But this I will surely affirm, that faith alone saved him. If he had lived and not regarded faith and the works of faith, he would have lost his salvation again. But this is what I am seeking to drive at: that faith by itself saved him, but works by themselves never justified anyone."[12]

Here you have heard the mind of St Chrysostom, from which you may perceive that faith is not without works (when it has opportunity to do them), and that works cannot get us to everlasting life without faith.

THE WORKS OF TRUE FAITH

There were three things in a previous sermon especially noted of living faith. Two of these have been declared to you. The first, was that faith is never idle, without good works, when occasion serves. The second, was that good works acceptable to God cannot be done without faith. Now to go forward to the third part, that is: what kind of works they are which spring out of true faith, and lead faithful people to everlasting life.

This can be best learned from our Saviour Christ himself, who was asked by a certain great man the same question: "What works shall I do," said a prince, "to come to everlasting life?" Jesus answered him, "If you want to come to everlasting life, keep the commandments." But the prince, not satisfied with this, asked further, "Which commandments?" (Luke 18:18-23; Matthew 19:16-18). The Scribes and Pharisees had made so many of their own laws and

---

12 Pseudo-Chrysostom, *De Fide et Lege Naturae* (PG 48:1081-1082). On the proper interpretation of the apparent idea here of losing salvation, see Null, *Thomas Cranmer's Doctrine of Repentance*, 224-227.

traditions, to bring people to heaven, besides God's commandments, that this man was in doubt about whether he should come to heaven by those laws and traditions or by the law of God, and therefore he asked Christ which commandments he meant. Christ answered him plainly, rehearsing the commandments of God, saying "You shall not kill. You shall not commit adultery. You shall not steal. You shall not bear false witness. Honour your father and your mother, and love your neighbour as yourself" (Matthew 19:18-19). By which words Christ declared that the laws of God are the very way that leads to everlasting life, and not the traditions and laws of people. So this is to be taken as a most true lesson taught by Christ's own mouth, that the works of the moral commandments of God are the very true works of faith, which lead to the blessed life to come.

Sin leads to idolatry

But people's blindness and malice, even from the beginning, has always been ready to fall from God's commandments. Adam, the first man, had but one commandment, that he should not eat of the forbidden fruit. Despite God's commandment, he gave credit to the woman, seduced by the subtle persuasion of the serpent, and so followed his own will, and left God's commandment. And ever since that time, everyone who has come from him has been so blinded through original sin, that they have always been ready to fall from God and his law, and to invent a new way to salvation by works of their own devising. Indeed, almost the whole world, forsaking the true honour of the only eternal living God, wandered about in their own fantasies: some worshipping the sun, the moon, and the stars; some Jupiter, Juno, Diana, Saturn, Apollo, Neptune, Ceres, Bacchus, and other dead men and women. Some were not satisfied with this, and worshipped diverse kinds of beasts, birds, fish, fowl, and serpents, with every country, town, and house being in a way divided, setting up images of such things as they liked, and worshipping them.

Such was the roughness of the people, after they fell to their own fantasies and left the eternal, living God and his commandments, that they devised innumerable images and gods. In which error and blindness they remained, until such time as Almighty God, pitying their blindness, sent his true prophet Moses into the world, to reprove and rebuke this extreme madness, and to teach the people to know the only living God and his true honour and worship.

But the corrupt inclination of mankind was so much given to follow their own fantasy, and (as we might say) to favour its own bird, that all the admonitions, exhortations, benefits, and threatenings of God could not keep them from such inventions. For despite all the benefits of God shown to the people of Israel, when Moses went up to the mountain to speak with Almighty God, he had been there only a few days when the people began to invent new gods. And as it came into their heads, they made a calf of gold, and knelt down and worshipped it (Exodus 32:1-6). And after that, they followed the Moabites, and worshipped Baal-peor the Moabites' God (Numbers 25:1-3).

Read the book of Judges, the book of the Kings, and the Prophets, and there you shall find how unsteadfast the people were, how full of inventions, and more ready to run after their own fantasies than God's most holy commandments. There shall you read of Baal, Moloch, Chemosh, Milcom, Baal-peor, Ashtaroth, Bel, the Dragon, Priapus, the brazen Serpent, the twelve signs, and many others, to whose images the people with great devotion invented pilgrimages, preciously adorning and censing them, kneeling down and offering to them, thinking this a high merit before God and to be esteemed above the precepts and commandments of God.[13]

---

13 See Numbers 25:1-3; Judges 2:13; 1 Kings 11:5, 7, 33; 2 Kings 18:4 (with Numbers 21:8-9 and John 3:14); 2 Kings 23:4-5, 13; 2 Kings 17:16, 21:3, 5, Isaiah 47:9, 13, Jeremiah 19:13, 27:9, and Zephaniah 1:5 on sorcery and "the twelve signs" of the zodiac (with Deuteronomy 18:10-11); Hosea 9:10; Amos 5:26; and the apocryphal book *Bel and the Dragon*. For Priapus, see 1 Kings 15:13 and 2 Chronicles 15:16 in the Vulgate (from the Hebrew *Asherah*).

Although at that time God commanded no sacrifice to be made except only in Jerusalem, they did the exact opposite and made altars and sacrifices everywhere, in hills, in woods, and in houses, not regarding God's commandments but esteeming their own fantasies and devotions to be better than them. And these errors were so spread abroad, that not only the uneducated people, but also the priests and teachers of the people were corrupted, partly by glory and covetousness and partly, by ignorance, blindly deceived with the same abominations. Things were so bad that King Ahab had only Elijah as a true teacher and minister of God, but eight hundred and fifty priests who persuaded him to honour Baal and Asherah and to sacrifice to them in the woods or groves (1 Kings 18:19-22). And so continued that horrible error, until the three noble Kings—Jehoshaphat, Hezekiah, and Josiah—God's chosen ministers, clearly destroyed them and brought the people back from such false inventions to the very commandments of God. For this, their immortal reward and glory remains and shall remain with God for ever (2 Chronicles 17:3-6, 30:14, 31:1, 34:3-7).

HUMAN TRADITIONS

Besides these inventions already mentioned, people's inclination to have their own holy devotions devised new sects and religious groups, called Pharisees, Sadducees, and Scribes. They had many holy and godly traditions and ordinances (as it seemed by the outward appearance, and the great glistening of their works), but in fact they all tended to idolatry, superstition, and hypocrisy. Their hearts within were full of malice, pride, covetousness, and all wickedness. Against these sects and their pretended holiness, Christ cried out more strongly than he did against any other people, saying and often rehearsing these words "Woe to you, Scribes and Pharisees, you hypocrites! For you clean the vessel on the outside, but within you are full of greed and filthiness. You blind Pharisee, and hypocrite! First make the inward part clean" (Matthew 23:25-26). For despite all their great traditions and outward shows of good works, devised by their own imagination, by which they appeared to the world as the most religious and holy people, Christ (who saw their hearts) knew that they were inwardly, in the sight of God, most unholy, most abominable, and the furthest away from God of all people. Therefore he said to them "Hypocrites! The Prophet Isaiah truly spoke of you when he said 'This people honour me with their lips, but their heart is far from me. Those who teach merely human doctrines and commandments, worship me in vain.' For you leave the commandments of God, to keep your own traditions" (Matthew 15:6-9. Isaiah 29:13).

Although Christ said, "They worship God in vain, who teach merely human doctrines and commandments", he did not mean by this to overthrow all human commandments; for he himself was always obedient to rulers and their laws, which are made for good order and governance of the people. But he reproved the laws and traditions made by the Scribes and Pharisees, which were not made only for the good order of the people (as the civil laws were) but were set up so high that they were made out to be for the right and pure worshipping of God, as if they were equal with God's laws, or above them. For many of God's laws could not be kept, but were compelled to give way to their rules.

This arrogance God detested, that people should so advance their laws, to make them equal with God's laws in which the true honouring and right worshipping of God consists, and to make his laws for them to be left aside. God has appointed his laws so we can honour what pleases him. His pleasure is also that all human laws which are not contrary to his laws, shall be obeyed and kept, as good and necessary for every Commonwealth, but not as things in which his honour principally rests. And all civil and human laws, either are or should be made to help people better keep God's laws, so that God should be better honoured by them. However, the Scribes and Pharisees were not content that their laws should be no higher esteemed than other positive and civil laws, nor would they allow them to be considered like other temporal laws. They called them holy and godly traditions, and would have them esteemed not only for a right and true worshipping of God (as God's laws indeed are), but also for the most high honouring of God, to which the commandments of God should give place. And for this reason, Christ so strongly spoke against them, saying, "Your traditions which people think of so highly are an abomination before God" (Luke 16:15).

It is common with such traditions that they lead to the transgression or breaking of God's commandments, and to more devotion in keeping the traditions and a greater conscience about breaking them, than concern for the commandments of God. The Scribes and Pharisees so superstitiously and scrupulously kept the Sabbath that they were offended with Christ because he healed sick people on it, and with his apostles because they being very hungry, gathered the ears of corn to eat on that day, and because his disciples did not wash their hands as often as the traditions required (Matthew 12:1-14). The Scribes and Pharisees quarrelled with Christ saying, "Why do your disciples break the traditions of the elders?" But Christ objected that in order to keep their own traditions they taught people to break the very commandments of God. For they taught the people such a devotion that they offered their goods into the treasure house of the Temple, under the pretence of honouring God, but left their fathers and mothers (to whom they were chiefly bound) unhelped. And so they broke the commandments of God, to keep their own traditions (Matthew 15:1-6. Mark 7:9). They esteemed an oath made by the gold or offering in the Temple, more than an oath made in the name of God himself, or of the Temple (Matthew 23:16-22).

They were more studious to pay their tithes of small things, than to do the greater things commanded of God, such as works of mercy, or to do justice, or to deal sincerely, uprightly, and faithfully with God and people. These (says Christ) ought to be done, and the other not left undone. And in short, they were of so blind judgment, that they stumbled at a straw, and leaped over a block. They would (as it were) carefully take a fly out of their cup, but drink down a whole camel (Matthew 23:23). And therefore Christ called them blind guides, warning his disciples from time to time to avoid their doctrine (Matthew 23:24). For although they seemed to the world to be most perfect people, both in living and teaching, yet their life was but hypocrisy, and their doctrine sour yeast, mingled with superstition, idolatry, and preposterous judgment, setting up human traditions and ordinances, in place of God's commandments.

THE WORKS OF FALSE RELIGION

So that everyone might rightly judge of good works, it has been declared in the second part of this sermon, what kind of good works God would have his people to walk in, namely such as he has commanded in his holy scripture, and not such works as people have invented out of their own brains, from a blind zeal and devotion, without the word of God. By mistaking the nature of good works, mankind has most highly displeased God, and has moved away from his will and commandments. So you have heard how much the world, from the beginning until Christ's time, was always ready to fall from the commandments of God, and to seek other means to honour and serve him, by means of a devotion created out of their own heads. And you have heard how people set up their own traditions, as high or above God's commandments, which has happened also in our times (which is more to be lamented) no less than it did among the Jews, and that by the corruption or at least by the negligence of those who chiefly ought to have preserved the pure and heavenly doctrine left by Christ.

What person, having any judgment or learning joined with a true zeal for God, does not see and lament that such false doctrine, superstition, idolatry, hypocrisy, and other enormities and abuses have entered into Christ's religion? Little by little, through such sour yeast, the sweet bread of God's holy word has been much hindered and laid aside. The Jews in their blindness never had so many pilgrimages to images, nor indulged in so much kneeling, kissing, and censing of them as has been used in our time. Sects and false religions were only ever a small minority among the Jews,[14] and were not as superstitiously abused in an ungodly way as they have been recently among us.

Such sects and religions had so many hypocritical and pretended works in their state of religion (as they arrogantly named it) that their lamps (as they said) always ran over, able to satisfy not only for their own sins but also for all their other benefactors and religious brothers and sisters, as they had persuaded the multitude of ignorant people in their ungodly and crafty way. In various places they kept merit markets, full of their holy relics, images, shrines, and works of overflowing abundance ready to be sold. And all things which they had were called holy—holy cowls,[15] holy girdles, holy pardons, holy beads, holy shoes, holy rules— and all full of holiness. And what thing can be more foolish, more superstitious, or ungodly, than for men, women, and children, to wear a Friar's coat to supposedly deliver them from fevers or pestilence? Or when they die, or when they are buried, to cause such a thing to be cast upon them, in the hope of being saved by this? Thanks be to God, this superstition has been little used in this realm, but in various other countries it has been, and is still used among many, both educated and uneducated.[16]

SUPERSTITIOUS MONASTIC VOWS
We must pass over the innumerable superstitions that there have been in strange apparel, in silence, in Dormitory, in Cloister, in Chapter, in choice of meats and drinks, and in such like things. Rather, let us consider what enormities and abuses have been in

---

14 Literally: "neither the fortieth part so many among the Jews", i.e. about 2.5%.

15 i.e. a monk's hooded cloak.

16 See William Nicholson (ed.), *The Remains of Edmund Grindal* (Cambridge: Cambridge University Press, 1843), 30 for mention of this practice in a funeral sermon from 1564, and John Ayre (ed.), *Prayers and Other Pieces of Thomas Becon* (Cambridge: Cambridge University Press, 1844), 518 for a similar mention from 1563.

the three chief principal points, which they called the three essentials or three chief foundations of religion, that is to say, obedience, chastity, and wilful poverty.

First, under the pretence or colour of obedience to their "father in religion" (which obedience they made themselves) they were made free by their rule and Canons from obedience to their natural father and mother, and from obedience to Emperor and King and all temporal power—whom by God's law they were very much duty bound to obey. And so by professing who they were not bound to obey, they forsook their due obedience.

And it would be better to pass over in silence how their profession of chastity was kept, and let the world judge of that which is well known, rather than with unchaste words to express their unchaste life, and therefore offend chaste and godly ears. And as for their wilful poverty, when they had possessions, jewels, plate, and riches they were equal or above merchants, gentlemen, Barons, Earls, and Dukes. Yet by this subtle term of sophistry, *proprium in commune*, that is to say, *proper in common*, they mocked the world, claiming that despite all their possessions and riches they were keeping their vow, and were in wilful poverty.[17]

But for all their riches, they might never help father nor mother, nor others who were indeed very needy and poor, without the permission of their father Abbot, Prior, or Warden. They might take from anyone, but they should not give anything to anyone, no not even to those whom the laws of God bound them to help. And so through their traditions and rules, they resisted the laws of God. And, therefore, what Christ said to the Pharisees might be most truly said of them: "You break the commandments of God by your traditions. You honour God with your lips, but your hearts are far from him" (Matthew 15:3, 8). And they prayed longer prayers by

---

17 See the similar attacks on monastic views in William Tyndale's exposition of Matthew 7:15-20 (from 1532) where he talks about some who say "I have no goods, nor any thing proper, or that is mine own. It is the convent's." Henry Walter (ed.), *Expositions and Notes on Sundry Portions of the Holy Scriptures… by William Tyndale* (Cambridge: Cambridge University Press, 1849), 124.

day and by night, under pretence or colour of such holiness, to get the favour of widows and other simple folks, that they might sing trentals,[18] and hold services for their husbands and friends, and admit or receive them into their prayers. This confirms the saying of Christ about them, "Woe to you, Scribes and Pharisees, hypocrites! For you devour widows' houses, under colour of long prayers: therefore your damnation shall be the greater. Woe to you, Scribes and Pharisees, hypocrites! For you travel by sea and by land to make more Novices, and new brethren, and when they are let in, or received into your sect, you make them the children of hell, worse than your yourselves are" (Matthew 23:14-15).[19]

May God be honoured, for putting light in the heart of his faithful and true minister of most famous memory, King Henry VIII, and giving him the knowledge of his word and an earnest affection to seek his glory, and to put away all such superstitious and Pharisaical sects invented by Antichrist and set up against the true word of God and the glory of his most blessed name, just as he gave the same spirit to the most noble and famous Princes, Jehoshaphat, Josiah, and Hezekiah. God grant all of us, the King's faithful and true subjects, to feed on the sweet and savoury bread of God's own word, and (as Christ commanded) to avoid all Pharisaical yeast of human false religion. Although that was, before God, most abominable and contrary to God's commandments and Christ's pure religion, it was praised as a most godly life, and the highest state of perfection—as though a person might be more godly, and more perfect by keeping human rules, traditions, and professions than by keeping the holy commandments of God.

---

18   A series of thirty Requiem Masses, sung on consecutive days or all at once on behalf of a dead person.

19   Matthew 23:14 does not appear in modern versions of the Bible such as the ESV or NIV, because it seems to be an unoriginal insertion derived from similar statements in Mark 12:40 and Luke 20:47, and does not appear in the earliest and best manuscripts of Matthew. It did appear in early modern English translations such as the KJV and that by William Tyndale. See Bruce Metzger, *A Textual Commentary on the Greek New Testament, Second Edition* (London: United Bible Societies, 1994), 50.

Roman Catholic Abuses

And briefly to pass over the ungodly and counterfeit religion, let us rehearse some other kinds of Roman Catholic superstitions and abuses, such as Beads,[20] Lady Psalters,[21] and Rosaries, Fifteen Os,[22] St Bernard's Verses,[23] St Agatha's Letters,[24] Purgatory, Masses satisfactory,[25] Stations,[26] Jubilees,[27] pretended relics, or hallowed beads, bells, bread, water, psalms, candles, fire, and other such things. We could speak of superstitious fastings, of fraternities or brotherhoods, of pardons, and other such merchandise, which were so esteemed and abused to the great prejudice of God's glory and commandments, that they were made most high and most holy things, by which to attain to everlasting life, or the cancellation of sin. Indeed, vain inventions, unfruitful ceremonies, and ungodly laws, decrees, and councils of Rome were in such a way advanced that nothing was thought comparable in authority, wisdom, learning, and godliness to them. So that the laws of Rome (as they said)

---

20 Rosary beads.

21 This consists of saying the *Ave Maria* (Hail Mary) one hundred and fifty times, with each group of 10 separated by the saying of the Lord's Prayer, and the Apostles' Creed said every fifty.

22 Prayers addressed to Jesus beginning "O Jesus" or "O Lord" after the pattern attributed to St Birgitta of Sweden (1303-1373), which also included recitations of the Lord's Prayer, the Creed, and the *Ave Maria*.

23 From a legend that the devil told St Bernard of Clairvaux (1090-1153) that if he daily said these eight (or twelve) verses it would protect him from death and he would know the day on which he was going to die.

24 St Agatha (martyred c. 252) was from Catania in Sicily. The legend is that a year after her death (5th February) her veil protected the town from an eruption of Mount Etna. So these "St Agatha's Letters" are most probably charms made annually on that day to supposedly protect houses from fire or other natural disasters.

25 That is, Masses which where the priest was said to offer Christ as a satisfaction for the sins of someone who had died. Article 31 calls these "blasphemous fables and dangerous deceits."

26 Probably the so-called the Stations of the Cross.

27 Years of Jubilee, for cancellation of sins. Cf. *Prayers and Other Pieces of Thomas Becon*, 518.

were to be received by everyone like the four Evangelists,[28] and all the laws of Princes must give way to them. And the laws of God were also partly left aside, and less esteemed, so that these laws, decrees, and councils with their traditions and ceremonies might be more duly kept, and had in greater reverence.

Thus were the people so blinded through ignorance with the godly show and appearance of those things, that they thought the keeping of them to be a more holy, a more perfect service and honouring of God, and more pleasing to God, than the keeping of God's commandments. Such has been the corrupt inclination of mankind, ever superstitiously given to make new ways of honouring God out of their own heads, and then to have more affection and devotion to keep those than to search out God's holy commandments and to keep them. And, furthermore, to take God's commandments for human commandments, and human commandments for God's commandments, indeed, for the highest and most perfect and holy of all God's commandments. And so was all confused, so that only a few well-educated people, and but a small number of them, knew or at the least wanted to know and affirm the truth, to separate or sever God's commandments from human commandments. And so grew much error, superstition, idolatry, vain religion, preposterous judgment, great contention, with all ungodly living.

TRULY HONOURING GOD

Therefore, as you have any zeal to rightly and purely honour God, as you have any regard to your own souls, and to the life that is to come which is both without pain and without end—apply yourselves chiefly above all things to read and hear God's word. Mark diligently in it what his will is, and with all your effort apply yourselves to follow that. First, you must have an assured faith in God, and give yourselves wholly to him. Love him in prosperity and adversity, and dread to offend him evermore. Then for his

---

28   That is, like the Gospels.

sake love all people, friends and foes, because they are his creation and image, and redeemed by Christ as you are. Consider in your minds how you may do good to all, as you are able, and hurt no one. Obey all your superiors, and governors, serve your masters faithfully and diligently, as well in their absence as in their presence, not for dread of punishment only, but for conscience sake, knowing that you are bound so to do by God's commandments.

Do not disobey your fathers and mothers, but honour them, help them, and please them as you are able to. Do not oppress others, or kill or beat them, neither slander nor hate anyone. But love all people, speak well of all, help and assist everyone, as you can, indeed, even your enemies who hate you, who speak evil of you, and who hurt you. Take no-one's goods, nor covet your neighbour's goods wrongfully, but content yourselves with that which you obtain lawfully. And also bestow your own goods charitably, as need requires.

Flee all idolatry, witchcraft, and perjury. Commit no kind of adultery, fornication, or other impurity, in will nor in deed, with anyone else's spouse or otherwise. And labouring continually during this life to thus keep the commandments of God (in which consists the pure, principal, and right honour of God and which, done in faith, God has ordained to be the right course and pathway to heaven), you shall not fail, as Christ has promised, to come to that blessed and everlasting life, where you shall live in glory and joy with God forever—to whom be praise, honour and dominion, for ever and ever. *Amen.*

HOMILY 6

CHRISTIAN LOVE

Of all the things that are good to be taught to Christian people, there is nothing more necessary to be spoken about and daily recalled than charity.[1] All kinds of works of righteousness are contained within it, just as the decay of it is the ruin of the world, the banishment of virtue, and the cause of all vice. Almost everyone thinks of themselves as loving, in their own way, and however detestable their life may be, to both God and people, they persuade themselves that they still have such love. Therefore, you shall hear now a true and plain description of love, not out of human imagination but from the very words and example of our Saviour Jesus Christ. In this description, everyone may consider themselves (as in a mirror), and see plainly without error whether they are truly loving, or not.

WHOLEHEARTED LOVE
Love means to love God with all our heart, all our soul, and all our powers and strength (Deuteronomy 6:5). *With all our heart*: that is to say, that our hearts and minds are set to believe his word, to trust

---

1   The word "charity" was often used in the sixteenth century to translate the New Testament Greek word ἀγάπη (*agape*), in passages such as 1 Corinthians 13. This is now more normally translate d as "love" rather than charity, because the latter can conjure up images of financial handouts to those of lesser status, or organised aid (from "charities"), which is not the main focus of the biblical word. I have often substituted love in the text here to make this clearer to modern readers.

*   The original title of this Homily was *A Homily of Christian Love and Charity*.

in him, and to love him above all other things that we love best in heaven or in earth. *With all our life*: that is to say, that our chief joy and delight is set on him and his honour, and our whole life is given to the service of God above all things, with him to live and die, and to forsake all other things, rather than him. For the one who loves their father or mother, son or daughter, house, or land, more than me (says Christ) is not worthy to have me (Matthew 10:37, 16:24-27, 19:29). *With all our power*: that is to say, that our hands and feet, our eyes and ears, our mouths and tongues, and all our parts and powers both of body and of soul, should be given to the keeping and fulfilling of his commandments.

This is the first and principal part of love, but it is not the whole. For charity is also to love everyone, good and evil, friend and foe, and whatever cause is given to the contrary, nevertheless to bear good will to everyone. Love is to behave ourselves well towards others in words as well as in all our outward acts and deeds. For this is what Christ himself taught, and also how he himself lived.

Concerning love for God, Jesus taught thus to a doctor of the law who asked him which was the greatest and chief commandment in the Law: "Love the Lord your God with all your heart, with all your soul, and with all your mind" (Matthew 22:37). And of the love that we ought to have among ourselves for each other, he teaches us this: "You have heard it taught in the past, 'You shall love your friend, and hate your foe.' But I tell you, love your enemies, speak well of those who defame you and speak evil of you. Do well to those who hate you, and pray for those who vex and persecute you, so that you may be the children of your father in heaven. For he makes his sun to rise on both the evil and the good, and sends rain to the just and the unjust. For if you love those who love you, what reward shall you have? Do not the tax collectors do likewise? And if you speak well only of those who are your brethren and dear beloved friends, are you doing more than others? Do not even pagans do that?" (Matthew 5:43-47). These are the very words of our Saviour Christ himself, concerning the love of our neighbour.

CHRIST'S LOVE FOR ENEMIES

The Pharisees (with their most troublesome traditions and false interpretations and glosses) had corrupted and almost clearly stopped up this pure well of God's living word. They taught that this love and charity applied only to one's friends, and that it was sufficient for someone to love those who love them, and hate their enemies. Therefore, Christ opened this well again, purged it and scoured it by giving a true and clear interpretation to his godly law of charity, which is this: that we ought to love everyone, both friend and foe, adding to this what benefit we shall have as a result, and what disadvantages from doing the contrary. What better thing could we wish for ourselves than for the eternal heavenly Father to adopt and accept us as his children? And this we shall be sure of, says Christ, if we love every person without exception. And if we do otherwise, he says, we are no better than the Pharisees, tax collectors, and unbelievers, and shall have our reward with them—that is, to be shut out from the number of God's chosen children, and from his everlasting inheritance in heaven.

In this way, Christ taught about true love that everyone is bound to love God above all things, and to love every person, both friend and foe. And this, he himself did: exhorting his adversaries, rebuking the faults of his adversaries, and when he could not amend them, yet he prayed for them.

First he loved God his Father above all things, so much that he sought not his own glory and will, but the glory and will of his Father. "I do not seek," he said "my own will, but the will of him who sent me" (John 5:30). Nor did he refuse to die, to satisfy his Father's will, saying "If it is possible, let this cup of death be taken from me. But if not, your will be done, and not mine" (Matthew 26:39, 42). He loved not only his friends, but also his enemies who (in their hearts) nursed an exceedingly great hatred against him, and with their tongues spoke all evil about him, and in their acts and deeds pursued him with all their might and power, even to death. Yet despite all this, he did not withdraw his favour from them, but still loved them, preached to them in love, rebuked their false doctrine, their wicked living, and did good to them, patiently enduring whatever they spoke or did against him. When they gave him evil words, he gave no evil in return. When they struck him, he did not strike them back. And when he suffered death, he did not slay them, nor threaten them, but prayed for them, and referred all things to his Father's will. As a sheep that is led to the slaughter, and as a lamb that is shorn of his fleece makes no noise or resistance, even so he went to his death, without any resistance, or opening his mouth to say any evil (Isaiah 53:7. Acts 8:32).

So, I have described to you what love is, both in terms of doctrine and in terms of the example of Christ himself. From this, everyone may without error know themselves, what state and condition they are in, whether they are loving (and so the child of the Father in heaven) or not. For although almost everyone persuades themselves that they are loving, let them examine no-one else but themselves, their own heart, their life, and their behaviour, and they shall not be deceived but truly discern and judge whether they are loving or not. For the one who does not follow their own appetite and will, but gives themselves earnestly to God to do all his will and commandments—they may be sure that they love God above all things, or else surely he loves them not, whatever they pretend. As Christ said, "If you love me, keep my commandments. For whoever knows my commandments, and keeps them, they are the one who loves me" (John 14:15, 21). And again he says, "The one who loves me will keep my word, and my Father will love them, and we will both come to them, and dwell with them. But the one who does not love me will not keep my words" (John 14:23-24). In the same way, the one who has a good heart and mind, and uses their tongue well, and does good deeds to everyone, friend and foe—they may know by this that they have love. And then they are sure that Almighty God accepts them as his dearly beloved children. As St John says, "This is how we can know who the children of God are, and who the children of the Devil are: whoever does not do what is right is not God's child, and neither is anyone who does not love their brother and sister" (1 John 3:10).

THE DIFFICULT ASPECTS OF LOVE

You have heard a plain and a fruitful description of charity, and how profitable and necessary a thing love is: how it stretches itself both to God and people, friend and foe, by the doctrine and example of Christ. You have also heard who may assure themselves whether they are loving people or not. Now let us continue on this same subject.

LOVE YOUR ENEMIES

The perverse nature of mankind, corrupted with sin and destitute of God's word and grace, thinks it against all reason that someone should love their enemy, and in many ways is persuaded against this. Against all such reasons, we ought to set the teaching as well as the living of our Saviour Christ who, loving us when we were his enemies, teaches us to love our enemies. He patiently endured many reproaches for us, suffered beating, and most cruel death. Therefore, we are not members of him if we will not follow him. Christ, says St Peter, suffered for us, leaving an example that we should follow him (1 Peter 2:21).

Furthermore, we must consider that to love our friends is no more than thieves, adulterers, murderers, and all wicked people do. Jews, Muslims, non-believers, and even all brute beasts love those who are their friends, those from whom they earn their living, or get any other benefits. But to love enemies is the proper condition of those who are the children of God, the disciples and followers of Christ.

The disobedient and corrupt nature of people ponders deeply

and repeatedly the offence and displeasure done to them by their enemies, and thinks it an intolerable burden to be bound to love those who hate them. But the burden should be easy enough if (on the other side) everyone would consider what displeasure they have done to their enemy in return, and what pleasure they have received from this. And if we find no equal or fair compensation, either in receiving such pleasure or in giving displeasure to them in return, then let us ponder the displeasures which we have given to Almighty God, how often and how grievously we have offended him.

If we wish to have God's forgiveness, there is no other remedy but to forgive the offences done to us, which are very small in comparison to our offences against God. And if we consider that the one who has offended us does not deserve to be forgiven by us, let us consider again that we deserve far less to be forgiven by God. And although our enemy does not deserve to be forgiven for their own sake, yet we ought to forgive them for God's love, considering how great and many benefits we have received from him, without deserving them, and that Christ expects us, for his sake, to forgive them their trespasses committed against us.

LOVE CHERISHES AND CORRECTS

Here there may arise a question that needs to be solved. If love requires us to think, speak, and do well to everyone, both good and evil, how can officers of the law execute justice on criminals or evildoers with love? How can they put evil people in prison, take away their goods, and sometimes their lives, according to laws, if love will not suffer them to do so?

Here is a plain and a brief answer: plagues and punishments are not necessarily evil of themselves. To an evil person they are both good and necessary, and may be executed according to love, and with love should be executed.

To speak of this further, you must understand that love has two roles, the one contrary to the other, and yet both are necessary for people of different sorts and dispositions. One role of love is to cherish good and innocent people, not to oppress them with false accusations but to encourage them with rewards to do well and to continue in well doing, defending them with the sword from their adversaries. Just as the office of bishops and pastors is to praise good people for doing good, that they may continue to do so, and to rebuke and correct by the word of God the offences and crimes of all those who are disposed to do evil.

The other role of love is to rebuke, correct, and punish vice, without regard for people's position or status, and is only to be used against those who are evil, and criminals or evildoers. It is as much the role of love to rebuke, punish, and correct those who are evil, as it is to cherish and reward those who are good and innocent. St Paul declares to the Romans that the governing authorities are ordained by God, not to be a terror to those who do right, but to those who do wrong, to draw the sword to take vengeance against the one who commits the sin (Romans 13:1-4). And St Paul bids Timothy strongly and earnestly to rebuke sin by the word of God (1 Timothy 5:20). Both offices should be diligently executed, to fight against the kingdom of the devil: the preacher with the word, and the governors with the sword. Otherwise, they neither love God, nor those whom they govern, if (for lack of correction) they wilfully suffer God to be offended, and those whom they govern to perish.

Every loving father corrects his natural son when he does something wrong, or else he does not love him. In the same way, all governors of realms, countries, towns, and houses should lovingly correct those under their governance who are offenders, and cherish those who live innocently—if they have any respect to God and their office, or love for those they govern. Such rebukes and punishments of those who offend, must be done in reasonable time, otherwise the offenders fall headlong into all kinds of mischief, and are not only evil themselves, but also do harm to many others, drawing them by their evil example to sin and outrage after them. One thief may rob many people, and also make many thieves. One seditious person may allure many, and annoy a whole town or country. And love requires such evil people, who are great offenders against God and the commonwealth, to be cut from the body of the commonwealth, lest they corrupt other good and honest persons, like a good surgeon cuts away a rotten and festering limb because of the love they have for the whole body, lest it infect other limbs adjoining it.

Thus it is declared to you what true charity or Christian love is—so plainly, that no one should to be deceived. Whoever keeps this love, not only towards God (whom they are bound to love above all things) but also towards their neighbour, friend as well as foe—it shall surely keep them from all offending of God and people. Therefore note well this one short lesson: that by true Christian love, God ought to be loved above all, and all people ought to be loved too—good and evil, friend and foe. And we ought to do good to all, as we can: those who are good we ought to love, to encourage, and to cherish because they are good; and those who are evil we ought of love to procure and seek their correction and due punishment, so that they may by this either be brought to goodness, or at least that God and the commonwealth may be less hurt and offended.

If we thus direct our life, by Christian love and charity, then Christ promises and assures us that he loves us, that we are the children of our heavenly Father, reconciled to his favour, very members of Christ, and that after the short time of this present and mortal life, we shall have with him everlasting life in his everlasting kingdom of heaven. Therefore to him, with the Father and the Holy Spirit, be all honour and glory, now and for ever. *Amen.*

MAKING AND
BREAKING OATHS

So that his most holy name should be honoured and evermore magnified by the people, Almighty God commanded that no one should take his name in their mouth vainly. He threatened punishment to those who irreverently abuse it by swearing, perjury, and blasphemy. So that this commandment may be better known and kept, it shall be declared to you both how it is lawful for Christian people to swear an oath, and also what peril and danger it is vainly to swear such oaths, or to commit perjury.

LAWFUL OATHS
First, when judges require oaths of people for declaration of the truth or for execution of justice, this manner of swearing is lawful.[1] It is also lawful when people make faithful promises, calling to witness the name of God, to keep covenants, honest promises, statutes, laws, and good customs as Christian rulers do in their conclusions of peace, for the conservation of common wealth, and private persons promise their fidelity in marriage, or one to an-

---

1   Article 39 of *The Thirty-nine Articles* says: "As we confess that vain and rash Swearing is forbidden Christian men by our Lord Jesus Christ, and *James* his Apostle, so we judge, that Christian Religion doth not prohibit, but that a man may swear when the Magistrate requireth, in a cause of faith and charity, so it be done according to the Prophet's teaching, in justice, judgement, and truth." The end alludes to Jeremiah 4:2 which is expounded below.

*   The original title of this Homily was *A Homily against Swearing and Perjury*.

other in honesty and true friendship. It is lawful for all when they swear to keep common laws, and local statutes, and good customs, for due order to be had and continued among people. It is lawful when subjects swear to be true and faithful to their rulers and countries,[2] and when judges, magistrates, and officers swear truly to execute their offices. It is lawful when a person would affirm the truth in setting forth God's glory (for the salvation of the people) in open preaching of the gospel, or in giving good counsel privately for their soul's health.

All these ways of swearing, for necessary and honest causes, are lawful. But when people swear out of custom, in reasoning, buying and selling, or other daily communications (and many are common and great swearers) such swearing is ungodly, unlawful, and prohibited by the commandment of God. For such swearing is nothing else but the taking of God's holy name in vain.

Here it should be noted that *lawful* swearing is not forbidden, but commanded by Almighty God. For we have examples of Christ, and godly men, in holy scripture, who swore themselves and required oaths of others likewise. And God's commandment is, "You shall fear the Lord your God, and shall swear by his name" (Deuteronomy 6:13). And Almighty God says by his prophet David, "all who swear by God will glory in him" (Psalm 63:11). In this way our Saviour Christ swore several times, saying, "Truly truly" (e.g. John 3:3, 11). And St Paul swears thus: "I call God as my witness" (2 Corinthians 1:23). And Abraham (as he was getting old) required an oath of his servant, that he would find a wife for his son Isaac, who should come from his own kindred; and the servant swore that he would perform his master's will (Genesis 24:1-9). Abraham also swore to Abimelech the king of Gerar, when he required him to, that he would not hurt him or his posterity, and likewise did Abimelech swear to Abraham (Genesis

---

2   This originally read "King and Sovereign Lord", but it is common now for people to take oaths of allegiance to their rulers (who may not be kings) or to countries (or to trans-national Unions, or even to the flags of their countries).

21:22-31). And David swore to be and continue a faithful friend to Jonathan, and Jonathan swore to become a faithful friend to David (1 Samuel 18:3, 20:12-17, 42).

God once commanded that if a thing was given in pledge to someone, or left with them to keep, if the same thing were stolen or lost then the keeper of it should be sworn before judges, that they did not convey it away, or use any deceit in causing the same to be carried away, by their consent or knowledge (Exodus 22:10-11). And St Paul says that in all matters of controversy between two people, if one says yes and the other no, yet no due proof of the truth can be found, the end of every such controversy must be an oath administered by a judge (Hebrews 6:16).

MAKING OATHS RIGHTLY

God by the prophet Jeremiah says, "You shall swear, 'The Lord lives', in truth, in judgment, in righteousness" (Jeremiah 4:2). So that whoever swears when they are required to by a judge, let them be sure in their conscience that their oath has these three conditions, and they shall never need to be afraid of perjury. First, the one who swears may swear *truly*, that is, they must (setting apart all favour and affection to the parties involved) have the truth only before their eyes. For love of truth they must say and speak that which they know to be truth, and no further. Second, the one who takes an oath must do it *with judgment*, not rashly and unadvisedly, but soberly, considering what an oath is. Thirdly, the one who swears must swear *in righteousness*, that is, for the very zeal and love which they have for the defence of innocence, to the maintenance of the truth, and of the righteousness of the matter or cause. All profit, loss, all love and favour to the person for friendship or kindred should be laid aside.

Thus an oath (if it has with it these three conditions) is a part of God's glory, which we are bound by his commandments to give to him. For he wills that we shall swear only by his name, not that he has pleasure in oaths. In the same way as he commanded the Jews to offer sacrifices to him—not for any delight that he had in them, but to keep the Jews from committing idolatry—so he commands us to swear by his holy name, not to teach us that he delights in swearing, but that he forbids us to give his glory to any creature in heaven, earth, or water (Isaiah 42:8. Psalm 150:6). So lawful oaths are commanded by God, used by Patriarchs and Prophets, by Christ himself, and by his apostle Paul. Therefore, Christian people must think lawful oaths, both godly and necessary.

For by lawful promises and covenants confirmed by oaths, rulers and their countries are confirmed in common tranquillity and peace. By holy promises, with calling on the name of God to witness, we are made living members of Christ when we profess his religion, receiving the sacrament of baptism. By a similar holy promise, marriage knits together man and wife in perpetual love, so that they do not desire to be separated in any adversities. By lawful oaths, which rulers, judges, and magistrates swear, common laws are kept undamaged; justice is impartially administered; innocent persons, fatherless children, widows, and the poor are defended from murderers, oppressors, and thieves, so that they suffer no wrong or harm. By lawful oaths, mutual society, friendly relations, and good order are continually kept in all communities such as boroughs, cities, towns, and villages. And by lawful oaths, criminals are searched out, wrongdoers are punished, and those who sustain wrong are restored to their right. Therefore lawful swearing cannot be evil, since it brings to us so many godly, good, and necessary advantages.

ANSWERS TO EXCUSES
Therefore, when Christ so earnestly forbade swearing, it should not be understood as though he forbade all oaths. But he forbids all vain swearing and perjury both in the name of God, and in his creatures, such as the common use of swearing in buying, selling, and in our daily communication, to the intent that every Christian's word should be as well regarded in such matters as if

they should confirm their communication with an oath. For every Christian's word (says St Jerome) should be so true, that it should be regarded as an oath.[3] And Chrysostom witnessing the same says, "It is not appropriate to swear: for why do we need to swear when it is not lawful for one of us to lie to another?"[4]

Perhaps some will say, "I am compelled to swear, or else those who live with me, or buy and sell with me will not believe me." To this, St Chrysostom answered that whoever says this shows themselves to be an unjust and a deceitful person. For if they were a trustworthy person, and their deeds taken to agree with their words, they would not need to swear at all.[5] For the one who uses truth and plainness in their bargaining and communication shall have no need of such vain swearing to make themselves credible with their neighbours so they will not mistrust their words. If their credence is really so lost that they think no one will believe them without such oaths, then they may well think that their credibility has completely gone. For it is true (as Theophylact writes) that "no one is less trusted than the one who swears so much."[6] And Almighty God by the wise man says, "That person who swears much shall be full of sin, and the scourge of God shall not depart from their house".[7]

---

3   Jerome (342-420) was a Christian scholar from Stridon in what is now Croatia. See his *In Evangelium Matthaei* on Matthew 5:34-37 in St Jerome, *Commentary on Matthew* (translated by Thomas P. Scheck; Washington, D.C.: Catholic University of America Press, 2008), 83 (PL 26:40).

4   This is actually a quotation from St Chromatius (died 406/407), who was Bishop of Aquileia, Italy (perhaps confused with Chrysostom here and in other writers because of the abbreviation of their names to Chr). See Chromatius, *In Evangelium Matthaei*, 10.2 on Matthew 5:33-37 in PL 20:352 and Chromatius of Aquileia, *Sermons and Tractates on Matthew* (translated by Thomas P. Scheck; New York: Newman Press, 2018).

5   Chrysostom, *In Epistolam ad Ephesios*, 2.4 on Ephesians 1:11-14 (PG 62:21; NPNF 13:58).

6   Theophylact (c.1050-1107) was a Bible commentator and Archbishop of Ohrid in what is now North Macedonia. See his *Enarratio in Evangelium Matthaei* on Matthew 5:37 in *The Explanation by Blessed Theophylact of the Holy Gospel According to St Matthew* (translated by Christopher Stade; Manchester, MO: Chrysostom Press, 2006), 54 (PG 123:199-200).

7   From the apocryphal book of Sirach 23:11.

But here, some will excuse the many oaths in their daily talk by saying, "Why should I not swear, when I swear truly?" To such people it may be said that although they swear truly, yet in swearing often unadvisedly, for trifles, without necessity, and when they should not swear, they are not without fault, but take God's most holy name in vain. Much more ungodly and unwise are those who abuse God's most holy name, not only in buying and selling of small things daily in all places, but also in eating, drinking, playing, talking, and reasoning. As if none of these things might be done without commonly using and abusing the most holy name of God, vainly and irreverently talking and swearing. This breaks God's commandment and procures his indignation.

FALSE OATHS AND PERJURY

You have been taught in the first part of this sermon against swearing and perjury, what a great danger it is to use the name of God in vain. And that not every kind of swearing is unlawful or against God's commandment, but that there are three things required in a lawful oath. First, that it is made for the maintenance of the truth. Secondly, that it is made with judgment, not rashly and unadvisedly. Thirdly, that it is made for the zeal and love of justice. You heard also what benefits come from lawful oaths, and what danger comes from rash and unlawful oaths. Now concerning the rest of this subject, you shall understand that those who make lawful promises of good and honest things by an oath, but do not keep them, also use the name of God in vain. As do those who promise evil and unlawful things, and do perform those.

BREAKING OATHS AND MAKING BAD ONES

There are two notable punishments which we read of in scripture for those who do not regard their godly promises bound by an oath, but who wittingly and wilfully break them. First, Joshua and the people of Israel made a league and faithful promise of perpetual amity and friendship with the Gibeonites (Joshua 9:3-15).

Despite this, afterwards in the days of wicked Saul many of these Gibeonites were murdered, contrary to this faithful promise made. Almighty God was so very displeased with this, that he sent a universal famine on the whole country, which continued for the space of three years. And God would not withdraw his punishment until the offence was avenged by the death of seven sons or kinsmen of King Saul (2 Samuel 21:1-14).

Second, when Zedekiah, King of Jerusalem, promised fidelity to the King of Babylon, but afterwards (contrary to his oath and allegiance) rebelled against King Nebuchadnezzar: this unbelieving king, by God's permission and sufferance, invaded the land of Judah and, besieging the city of Jerusalem, compelled King Zedekiah to flee. And as Zedekiah fled, Nebuchadnezzar took him prisoner, slaughtered his sons before his face, and put out both his eyes; and binding him with chains, he led him as a prisoner miserably into Babylon (2 Kings 24:17-25:7). In this way, God shows plainly how much he abhors breakers of honest promises bound by an oath made in his name.

We also have examples in the scriptures of those who make wicked promises by an oath, and do carry them out: chiefly Herod, certain wicked Jews, and Jephthah. Herod promised by an oath to the girl who danced before him, to give her whatever she asked for. When she was instructed by her wicked mother to ask for the head of John the Baptist, Herod, as he had taken a wicked oath, so he more wickedly carried it out, and cruelly killed the most holy prophet (Matthew 14:6-11). In the same way, some malicious Jews made an oath, cursing themselves if they either ate or drank, until they had slain St Paul (Acts 23:12). And Jephthah, when God had given to him victory over the children of Ammon, promised to God (in an act of foolish devotion) to offer for a sacrifice to him whatever came out of the doors of his house to meet him after his return home. By force of which foolish and ill-advised oath, he killed his one and only daughter, who came out of his house with mirth and joy to welcome him home (Judges 11:30-39). Thus the promise which he made (most foolishly) to God, against God's everlasting will and the law of nature, he most cruelly performed, thus committing against God a double offence.

Therefore, whoever makes any promise, binding themselves to it by an oath: let them be careful that the thing which they promise is good and honest, and not against the commandment of God, and that it is in their own power to perform it justly. And such good promises must all people assuredly always keep. But if someone at any time shall, either out of ignorance or out of malice, promise and swear to do any thing which is either against the law of Almighty God, or not in their power to perform: let them count it as an unlawful and ungodly oath.

AGAINST PERJURY

Now, we must also say something about perjury. So that you may know how great and grievous an offence against God wilful perjury is, I will show you what it is to take an oath before a judge upon a book.

First, people lay their hands on the gospel book, and swear truly to enquire and to make a true presentation of things they are charged with, and not to hold back from saying the truth, and doing truly, for favour, love, dread, or malice towards any person, as God and the holy contents of that book may help them. They must consider that in that book is contained God's everlasting truth, his most holy and eternal word, by which we have forgiveness of our sins and are made inheritors of heaven, to live for ever with God's angels and saints in joy and gladness. In the gospel book are also contained God's terrible threats to obstinate sinners who will not amend their lives or believe the truth of God's holy word, and the everlasting pain prepared in hell for idolaters, hypocrites, for false and vain swearers, for perjured people, for false witness bearers, for false condemners of the innocent and guiltless, and for those who for favour, hide the crimes of evildoers so that they are not punished.

So whoever wilfully lies and perjures themselves on Christ's holy gospel, utterly forsakes God's mercy, goodness, and truth, as well as the merits of our Saviour Christ's nativity, life, passion, death, resurrection, and ascension. They refuse the forgiveness of sins promised to all penitent sinners, the joys of heaven, and the company of angels and saints for ever. All these benefits and comforts are promised to true Christians in the gospel. But they, lying on the gospel, give themselves over to the service of the Devil—the master of all lies, falsehood, deceit, and perjury—provoking the great indignation and curse of God against them in this life, and the terrible wrath and judgment of our Saviour Christ at the great day of the last judgment, when he shall justly judge both the living and the dead, according to their works. For whoever forsakes the truth—for the love or displeasure of anyone, or for cash and profit to themselves—forsakes Christ and, with Judas, betrays him.

And even if such perjured people's falsehood is now kept secret, yet it shall be exposed at the last day, when the secrets of all our hearts shall be revealed to all the world. And then the truth shall appear, and accuse them; and their own conscience, with all the blessed company of heaven, shall bear witness truly against them. And Christ the righteous judge shall then justly condemn them to everlasting shame and death.

Almighty God by the prophet Malachi threatens to punish this sin of perjury severely, saying to the Jews, "I will come to you in judgment, and I will be a swift witness and a sharp judge against sorcerers, adulterers, and perjured persons" (Malachi 3:5). God also declared this to the prophet Zechariah in a vision, in which the prophet saw a book flying, which was twenty cubits long and ten cubits broad. God then said to him, "This is the curse that shall go forth on the face of the earth, for falsehood, false swearing, and perjury. And this curse shall enter into the house of the false person and into the house of the perjured person, and it shall remain in the midst of their house, and consume them, the timber and stones of their house" (Zechariah 5:1-4). Thus you see how much God hates perjury, and what punishment God has prepared for those who swear falsely, and perjured persons.

Thus you have heard, how and in what causes it is lawful for a Christian to swear an oath. You have heard what characteristics and conditions a lawful oath must have, and also how such lawful oaths are both godly and necessary to be observed. You have heard that it is not lawful to swear vainly—that is, to swear for other, lesser causes and in such ways as have been declared. And finally, you have heard how damnable a thing it is, either to perjure ourselves, or to keep an unlawful or an ill-advised oath. Therefore, let us earnestly pray for grace, that all vain swearing and perjury may be set aside, and we may only use such oaths as are lawful and godly, and that we may truly without all fraud keep them, according to God's will and pleasure—to whom, with the Son, and the Holy Spirit, be all honour and glory. *Amen.*

FALLING AWAY FROM GOD

The wise man said that pride was the first beginning of our falling away from God. For by it, our hearts are turned from God our maker: "For pride," he says, "is the fountain of all sin, and the one who has it shall be full of cursing, and at the end it shall overthrow them."[1] And as by pride and sin we go away from God, so shall God and all goodness with him go from us. The prophet Hosea plainly affirms that those who move away from God by living in vice, and yet would try to pacify him with sacrifices and satisfy him that way—they labour in vain. For, despite all their sacrifices, he will withdraw himself from them. For, says the prophet, they do not apply their minds to return to God; although they go about with whole flocks and herds to seek the Lord, yet they shall not find him, for he has withdrawn from them (Hosea 5:4-6).

HOW WE FALL AWAY

Now concerning our turning towards God or away from God, you must understand that it may be done in several different ways. Sometimes it is done directly by idolatry, as Israel and Judah did (Hosea 4:12, 5:5) Sometimes people fall away from God by lack

---

1   From the apocryphal book of Sirach 10:12-13.

*   The original title of this Homily was *A Sermon: How Dangerous a Thing it is to Fall from God*.

of faith, and mistrusting of God. Isaiah speaks about this in this way: "Woe to those who go down to Egypt to seek for help, trusting in horses and having confidence in the number of chariots and the power of horsemen. They have no confidence in the holy God of Israel, nor do they seek for the Lord." But what follows? "The Lord shall let his hand fall upon them, and down shall come both the helper, and the one who is helped: they shall be altogether destroyed" (Isaiah 31:1, 3).

Sometimes people move away from God by neglecting his commandments concerning their neighbours, which command them to express hearty love towards everyone, as Zechariah said to the people on God's behalf: "'Bring about true justice. Show mercy and compassion to one another. Do not oppress the widow or the orphan, the foreigner or the poor. Do not plot evil things against each other.' But they refused to listen; they stubbornly turned their backs and covered their ears. They made their hearts as hard as stone and would not listen to the Law, or to the words that the LORD Almighty sent by his Spirit through the earlier prophets. So the LORD Almighty was very angry. 'When I called, they did not listen; so when they called, I would not listen,' says the LORD Almighty. 'I scattered them with a whirlwind among all the nations that they did not know. The land they left behind was so desolate, that no one travelled through it. This is how they made the pleasant land desolate'" (Zechariah 7:9-14).

In short, all those who cannot abide the word of God, but follow the persuasions and stubbornness of their own hearts, go "backwards and not forwards" (as it is said in Jeremiah 7:24). They go and turn away from God. As Origen says, "The one who with mind, with study, with deeds, with thought and care applies and gives themselves to God's word, and thinks upon his laws day and night, and gives themselves wholly to God, and in his precepts and commandments is exercised: this is the one who is turned to God." And on the other side he says, "Whoever is occupied with fables and tales, when the word of God is rehearsed, they are turned away from God. Whoever in times of reading God's word is concerned in their mind with worldly business, with money or cash, they are turned away from God. Whoever is entangled by concern for possessions, filled with the covetousness of riches, and whoever works for the glory and honour of this world, they are turned away from God."[2] So in his view, whoever does not have a special concern for what is commanded or taught by God—the one who does not listen to it, embrace it, and print it in their heart, so that they may duly fashion their life after it—they are plainly turned away from God, even if they do other things out of their own mind and devotion, which to them seem better and more to God's honour.

We are taught and admonished in the holy scripture that this is true by the example of King Saul. He was commanded by God through Samuel that he should kill all the Amalekites and destroy them completely with their goods and cattle. But he, moved partly with pity, and partly (as he thought) with devotion for God, saved Agag the King, and all the best of their cattle, to make sacrifices to God with them. God was highly displeased with all this, and said to the Prophet Samuel, "I regret that I ever made Saul King, for he has forsaken me, and not followed my words." And so he commanded Samuel to confront him. When Samuel asked why (contrary to God's word) Saul had saved the cattle, he excused the matter: partly, by fear, saying he dared not do otherwise because the people wanted it so; and partly, because they were large beasts, he thought God would be content, seeing as it was done with a good intention and devotion to honour God by sacrificing them. But Samuel rebuked all such intentions and devotions because however much they may have seemed to be for God's honour, they were not in line with his word, by which we may be assured of his pleasure. So he said, "Does God want sacrifices and offerings? Or rather that his word should be obeyed? To obey him is better than

---

2   Origen, *In Exodum Homiliae*, Homily 12 on Exodus 34 §2. See Origen, *Homilies on Genesis and Exodus* (translated by Ronald E. Heine; Washington, D.C.: Catholic University of America Press, 1982), 367-374 (PG 12:383).

offerings, and to listen to him is better than offering the fat of rams: for rebellion against his voice is as evil as the sin of divination: and not to agree to it is like abominable idolatry. And now, because you have cast away the word of the Lord, he has cast away you, and rejected you as king" (1 Samuel 15:1-24).

How God turns away

By all these examples of holy scripture, we may know that if we forsake God, so shall he always forsake us. And a person can easily see from the terrible threatenings of God what a pitiable state consequently and necessarily follows on from this. And although someone may not grasp all that misery to its greatest extent, it being so great that it passes anyone's capacity in this life sufficiently to consider it; yet they shall soon perceive so much of it, that if their heart is not completely made of stone and harder than diamond, they shall fear, tremble, and quake, to call this to mind.

First, the displeasure of God towards us is commonly expressed in the scripture by these two things: by showing us a frightening face, or by turning his face and hiding it from us. By "showing his frightening face" is signified his great wrath; but "turning his face" or hiding it means that he clearly forsakes us, and gives us over. These ways of speaking about God are metaphors taken from human behaviour. For people usually have a good, cheerful, and loving face towards those whom they favour, so that from their face or countenance one can usually tell how they think or feel about others. So when God shows his dreadful countenance towards us, that is to say, he sends dreadful plagues of sword, famine, or pestilence on us, it appears that he is greatly angry with us. But when he withdraws from us his word, the right doctrine of Christ, his gracious assistance and aid (which is ever joined to his word), and leaves us to our own wit, our own will and strength: he declares then that he is beginning to forsake us.

God has shown to all those who truly believe his gospel, his face of mercy in Jesus Christ. This so lightens their hearts that they (if they see it as they ought to) are transformed into his image, are made partakers of the heavenly light and of his Holy Spirit, and are conformed to him in all the goodness necessary for the children of God. And if they afterwards neglect this, if they are ungrateful to him, if they do not order their lives according to his example and doctrine and to display his glory, he will take away from them his kingdom, his holy word, by which he should reign in them, because they do not produce the fruit of it that he looks for (Isaiah 5:1-7. Mark 12:1-11).

Nevertheless, God is so merciful, and so patient, that he does not bring upon us that great wrath suddenly. But when we begin to shrink from his word, not believing it or not expressing it in our lives, first he sends his messengers, the true preachers of his word, to admonish and warn us of our duty. He says that he, for his part, because of the great love he has for us, delivered his own Son to suffer death, that we by his death might be delivered from death and restored to the life everlasting, evermore to dwell with him and to be partakers and inheritors with him of his everlasting glory and kingdom of heaven. But he also says that we, for our parts, should walk in a godly life, as is appropriate for his children to do. And if this does not work, but we still remain disobedient to his word and will, not knowing him, nor loving him, not fearing him, not putting our whole trust and confidence in him; and on the other side, behaving ourselves uncharitably to our neighbours, by disdain, envy, malice, or by committing murder, robbery, adultery, gluttony, deceit, lying, swearing, or other similar detestable works and ungodly behaviour—then he warns us by terrible threatenings, swearing in his great anger that whoever does these works shall never enter into his rest, which is the kingdom of heaven (Hebrews 4:1-13. Galatians 5:21. Psalm 95:11).

THE STERN FROWN OF GOD

In the first part of this sermon, you have learned how many sorts of ways people fall away from God: some by idolatry, some for lack of faith, some by neglecting their neighbours, some by not hearing God's word, and some by the pleasure they take in the vanities of worldly things. You have also learned about the miserable condition of those who have gone from God; and how God, of his infinite goodness, to call people back from that his misery first uses gentle warnings from his preachers, and afterwards lays on terrible threatenings.

GOD'S FRIGHTENING FACE

Now if this gentle warning and threatening together does not work, then God will show his frightening face to us.[3] He will pour intolerable plagues on our heads, and afterwards he will take away all his aid and assistance from us, with which he used to defend us from all such calamities. As the evangelical prophet Isaiah teaches us, agreeing with Christ's parable, God had made a great vineyard for his beloved children, and he hedged it, walled it round about, planted it with chosen vines, and made a turret in the midst of it, and also a winepress. And when he looked for it to produce good grapes, it brought forth wild grapes. And afterwards it follows, "Now I will show you (says God) what I will do with my vineyard: I will pluck down the hedges, that it may perish. I will break down the walls that it may be trampled down. I will let it lie waste. It shall not be cut; it shall not be dug; but briers and thorns shall overgrow it, and I shall command the clouds that they shall no more rain upon it" (Isaiah 5:1-6. Matthew 21:33-41).

By these threatenings we are admonished and warned that if we, who are the chosen vineyard of God, do not produce good

---

3   Literally, "his terrible countenance". I have used the word *frightening* instead of the Homily's "terrible, dreadful, or fearful" countenance, since the basic meaning is that this stern frown of God induces fear and reverence in us, not that it is bad or that he is full of fear, which some modern readers might misunderstand those terms to mean.

grapes (that is to say, good works that may be delectable and pleasant in his sight) when he looks for them and sends his messengers to call on us for them, but rather bring forth wild grapes (that is to say, sour works, unsavoury, and unfruitful): then he will pluck away all our defences, and permit grievous plagues of famine, battle, food shortages, and death, to come upon us.

Finally, if these do not work, he will let us lie waste; he will give us over; he will turn away from us; he will dig and clear no more around us; he will leave us alone, and allow us to produce whatever fruit we will—to bring forth brambles, briars, and thorns, all wickedness, all vice—and that so abundantly, that they shall completely overwhelm us, choke, strangle, and utterly destroy us.

FALSE FREEDOM

But those who do not live for God in this world, but for their own carnal liberty, do not perceive this great wrath of God towards them, that he will not dig or clear any more around them, and that he leaves them alone even to themselves. But they take this for a great benefit from God, to have all the freedom they like: and so they live, as if carnal liberty were the true liberty of the gospel. But God forbid (good people) that we should ever desire such liberty. For although God sometimes allows the wicked to have their pleasure in this world, yet the final end of ungodly living is eventually endless destruction.

The murmuring Israelites had what they longed for: they had quails enough, even until they were weary of them. But what was the end of the story? Their sweet meat had sour sauce: even while the meat was in their mouths, the plague of God came upon them, and suddenly they died (Numbers 11:4-6, 31-33; Psalm 78:30-31). So if we live in an ungodly way, and God allows us to follow our own wills, to have our own delights and pleasures, and does not correct us with some plague: he is undoubtedly almost utterly displeased with us.

Although God may take a while before he strikes, yet many

times when he strikes such people he strikes them at once for ever. So that when he does not strike us, when he ceases to afflict us, to punish or beat us, and permits us to run headlong into all ungodliness and the pleasures of this world that we delight in, without punishment and adversity—it is a dreadful token that he loves us no longer, that he cares for us no longer, but has given us over to our own selves. As long as someone prunes their vines, digs at the roots, and lays fresh earth around them, they are mindful of them and perceive some token of fruitfulness that may be recovered in them. But when he will no more lavish such cost or labour on them, then it is a sign that he thinks they will never be good. And a father, as long as he loves his child, is angry and corrects them when they do something wrong; but when that does not work, and so he ceases correcting them and allows them to do whatever they want—it is a sign that he intends to disinherit them and to cast them away for ever.

So surely nothing should pierce our heart so much, and make us feel so horribly afraid, as when we know in our conscience that we have grievously offended God, and continue to do so, and yet he strikes us not, but quietly allows us to continue in the wickedness that we delight in. Then especially it is time to cry and cry again, as David did: "Cast me not away from your presence, and take not your Holy Spirit from me" (Psalm 51:11); "Lord, do not turn away your face from me, do not cast your servant away in displeasure" (Psalm 27:9); "Hide not your face from me, or I will become like those who go down to hell" (Psalm 143:7). These prayers of lament certify for us what horrible danger those people are in, from whom God turns away (for the time being, and as long as he does so). They should also move and stir us to cry to God with all our heart, that we may not be brought into that state, which doubtless is so sorrowful, so miserable, and so dreadful, as no tongue can sufficiently express, nor any heart can think.

For what deadly grief may we suppose it is, to be under the wrath of God, to be forsaken by him, to have his Holy Spirit (the author of all goodness) taken away—to be brought to so vile a condition, that one shall be left fit for no better purpose than to be forever condemned in hell? For these Psalms of David show that when God turns his face away from anyone, they shall be left devoid of all goodness, and far from any hope of remedy. So also do the verses we saw before from Isaiah, which show that God, in the end, forsakes his unfruitful vineyard, and that he will not only permit it to bring forth weeds, briars, and thorns, but also punish the unfruitfulness of it. He says he will not prune it, he will not clear it, and he will command the clouds that they shall not rain upon it.

By this is signified the teaching of his holy word, which St Paul, in a similar way, expressed by planting and watering (1 Corinthians 3:6-8), meaning that he will take that away from them, so that they shall no longer be part of his kingdom. They shall no longer be governed by his Holy Spirit, and they shall be removed from the grace and benefits that they had, and ever might have enjoyed through Christ. They shall be deprived of the heavenly light and life which they had in Christ, while they remained in him. They shall be (as they were once) like people without God in this world (Ephesians 2:12), or rather in a worse condition. In short, they shall be given over to the power of the devil, who rules in all those who are cast away from God, as he did in Saul (1 Samuel 15:23-35, 16:14) and Judas (Luke 22:3; John 13:2, 27), and generally in all those who follow their own wills, the children of disobedience and unbelief (Ephesians 2:2; Colossians 3:6 KJV).

DESPERATION AND PRESUMPTION

Therefore, let us beware (good Christian people) in case we reject or cast away God's word (by which we obtain and retain true faith in God) and are not eventually cast off so far ourselves, that we become like children of unbelief. There are two kinds of such unbelief, quite different, indeed, almost complete opposites, and yet both are very far from returning to God. The first sort of people, only weighing their sinful and detestable living with the right judgment and straightness of God's righteousness, are so without counsel, and are so comfortless—as everyone from whom the Spirit of counsel (Isaiah 11:2) and comfort has gone must be—that they will not be persuaded in their hearts, but think that God cannot or will not take them again into his favour and mercy. The others, hearing the loving and large promises of God's mercy, but not properly understanding them, make those promises larger then God ever did, trusting that although they continue for a long time in their sinful and detestable living yet God, at the end of their life, will show his mercy to them, and that then they will return. And both of these two sorts of people are in a damnable state. And yet God (who does not desire the death of the wicked) has revealed the means by which both (if they take heed in good time) may escape (Ezekiel 18:23, 32, 33:11).

The first sort of people dread God's rightful justice in punishing sinners, by which they *should* be dismayed, and *should* indeed despair with regard to any hope that may be in themselves. But if they constantly or steadfastly believe that God's mercy is the remedy appointed for such despair and distrust, not only for them but generally for all who are sorry and truly repentant and will, through it all, stick to God's mercy—then they may be sure that they shall obtain mercy, and enter into the port or haven of safety. Whoever comes into this haven, however wicked they were before, they shall be out of danger of everlasting damnation, as God says by Ezekiel, "Whenever the wicked sinner returns in earnest and true repentance, I will forget all their wickedness" (Ezekiel 33:12, 14-16, 19).

The other sort of people are ready to believe God's promises, so they should be just as ready to believe the threatenings of God. They should believe the Law as well as the gospel, and that there is a hell and everlasting fire, as well as a heaven and everlasting joy. They should believe damnation is threatened to the wicked and evildoers, just as salvation is promised to the faithful in word and works, and that God is true in both of these things. And the sinners who continue in their wicked living ought to think that the promises of God's mercy and the gospel do not apply to them in that state, but only the Law and those scriptures which contain the wrath and indignation of God, and his threatenings. This should convince them that they too boldly presume on God's mercy and live over-indulgently, and so God more and more withdraws his mercy from them, and is eventually so provoked by them to wrath that he destroys such presumers, many times suddenly. For St Paul said this about such people: "When they say 'There is peace, there is no danger,' then sudden destruction shall come upon them" (1 Thessalonians 5:3).

Let us beware therefore of such wicked boldness to sin. For God, who has promised his mercy to those who are truly repentant (even at the very end) has not promised to the presumptuous sinner, either that they shall have long life, or that they shall have true repentance at the end. For that reason, he has made everyone's death uncertain, so that we should not put our hope in the hour of our death, and meanwhile (to God's high displeasure) live an ungodly life. Therefore, let us follow the counsel of the wise man, let us "not wait to turn back to the Lord", and let us "not postpone it day after day, for suddenly his wrath shall come, and in time of vengeance he will destroy the wicked."[4] Let us therefore turn now, and when we turn let us pray to God, as Hosea teaches, saying, "Forgive all our sins, and receive us graciously" (Hosea 14:2). And if we turn to him with a humble and a very penitent heart, he will receive us into his favour and grace, for his holy name's sake, for his promise's sake, and for the sake of his truth and mercy promised to all faithful believers in Jesus Christ his only natural Son—to whom, the only Saviour of the world, with the Father and the Holy Spirit, be all honour, glory, and power, forever and ever. *Amen.*

---

4   From the apocryphal book of Sirach 5:7.

HOMILY 9

THE FEAR OF DEATH

It is not to be marvelled at that worldly people are afraid to die. For death deprives them of all worldly honours, riches, and possessions, and the worldly person counts themselves happy with the fruit of these things, as long as they may enjoy them at their own pleasure. On the other hand, if they are dispossessed of such things without hope of recovery then they cannot but think of themselves as unhappy, because they have lost their worldly joy and pleasure. "Alas!" thinks this carnal person, "shall I now depart for ever from all my honours, all my treasures, from my country, friends, riches, possessions, and worldly pleasures, which are my joy and heart's delight? Alas that ever that day shall come when I must bid farewell to all of these at once, and never enjoy any of them again!" Therefore, it is not without great cause spoken by the wise man: "O death, how bitter and sour is the reminder of you to one who lives in peace and prosperity among their possessions, to someone living in comfort, living in their own way without trouble, pampered and well fed."[1]

There are other people, whom this world does not so greatly laugh at, but who are vexed and oppressed with poverty, sickness, or some other adversity. They fear death, partly because the flesh naturally abhors its own sorrowful end which death threatens them with, and partly, because of sicknesses and painful diseases

---

1   From the apocryphal book Sirach 41:1.

*   The original title of this Homily was *An Exhortation against the Fear of Death*.

which are very strong pains and agonies in the flesh, and commonly come to sick people before death, or at least accompany death when it comes.

THE SECOND DEATH

Although these two causes seem great and weighty to a worldly person, and move them to fear death, there is another far greater reason for them to fear death: and that is, the state and condition to which, at the last, death brings all those who have their hearts fixed on this world, without repentance and amendment. This state and condition is called "the second death" (Revelation 21:8), which shall follow for them all after this bodily death. And this is the death which ought really to be dreaded and feared. For it is an everlasting loss without remedy of the grace and favour of God and of everlasting joy and pleasure and happiness. It is not only the loss of these eternal pleasures forever, but also the condemnation of both body and soul, without appeal or hope of redemption, to everlasting pains in hell.

To this state, death sent the unmerciful and ungodly rich man whom Luke speaks of in his Gospel (Luke 16:19-31). He was living with all the wealth and pleasure in the world, and enjoying himself daily with luxury food and fine clothes. But he despised poor Lazarus, who lay pitifully at his gate and was miserably diseased and covered in sores and grievously afflicted with hunger. Both of these two men were stopped in their tracks by death, which led to the poor and miserable Lazarus being taken by the angels to Abraham's side, a place of rest, pleasure, and consolation. But the unmerciful rich man descended down into hell, and being in torment there he cried out for comfort, complaining of the intolerable pain that he suffered in that flame of fire—but it was too late. So to this place, bodily death sends all those who have their joy and happiness in this world, all those who in this world are unfaithful to God and uncharitable to their neighbours, and die without repentance and the hope of God's mercy. Therefore it is no marvel that worldly people fear death, for they have far greater cause to do so than they themselves even consider.

Thus we see three causes why worldly people fear death. One, because they shall lose their worldly honours, riches, possessions, and all their heart's desires when they die. Second, because of the painful diseases and bitter pangs which people commonly suffer either before or at the time of death. But the main cause above all others is the dread of that miserable state of eternal damnation both of body and soul, which they fear shall follow after they depart out of the worldly pleasures of this present life. For these causes, all mortals who are given to the love of this world are both in fear of death and in a state of death through sin (as the holy apostle says) so long as they live here in this world (Hebrews 2:15).

No fear in death
But—everlasting thanks be to Almighty God for ever!—there is never one of all these causes, no, nor all of them together, that can make a true Christian afraid to die—since they are truly members of Christ, the temple of the Holy Spirit, the children of God and true inheritors of the everlasting kingdom of heaven. On the contrary, they can see a great many causes, undoubtedly grounded upon the infallible and everlasting truth of the word of God, which move them to put away the fear of bodily death. They may even wish, desire, and heartily long for it, because of the manifold benefits and remarkable advantages which follow for every faithful person.

For death shall be to them no death at all, but truly a deliverance from death, and from all the pains, cares, and sorrows, miseries, and wretchedness of this world. It will truly be an entrance into rest, and a beginning of everlasting joy—a tasting of heavenly pleasures so great that no tongue is able to express, nor eye to see, nor ear to hear them, no, nor for any earthly person's heart to conceive them. Such are the exceedingly great benefits which God our heavenly Father, by his mere mercy and for the love of his Son, Jesus Christ, has laid up in store and prepared for those who humbly submit themselves to God's will and evermore sincerely love him from the bottom of their hearts!

We ought to believe that death, being slain by Christ, cannot keep anyone who steadfastly trusts in Christ under its perpetual tyranny and subjection. Rather, they shall rise again from death to glory at the last day appointed by Almighty God, just as Christ our head rose again, according to God's appointment, on the third day. For St Augustine says: "The head going before, the members trust they shall follow and come after."[2] And St Paul says, "If Christ is risen from the dead, we also shall rise from the dead" (1 Corinthians 15:20-23). And to comfort all Christian people in this, holy scripture calls this bodily death a sleep (John 11:11, 13; Acts 7:60; 1 Thessalonians 4:13-18), in which our senses are (as it were) taken from us for a while and yet, when we awaken, we are more fresh than we were when we went to bed.

THE DOORWAY TO LIFE

So although we have our souls separated from our bodies for a season, yet at the general resurrection we shall be more fresh, beautiful, and perfect than we are now. For now we are mortal, but then we shall be immortal. Now we are infected with various infirmities, but then we shall be completely free of all mortal infirmities. Now we are subject to all carnal desires, but then we shall be entirely spiritual, desiring nothing except God's glory and things eternal.

So this bodily death is a door or entrance into life, and therefore not so much dreadful (if it is rightly considered) as it is comfortable; not a mischief, but a remedy of all mischief; not an enemy but a friend; not a cruel tyrant but a gentle guide, leading us not to mortality but to immortality, not to sorrow and pain but to joy and pleasure which endures forever. If death is gratefully received and accepted as God's messenger and we patiently bear it for the

---

2   See Pusey (ed.), *Expositions on the Book of Psalms by S. Augustine*, 3:271 (PL 36:786) on Psalm 66 §1 commenting on Colossians 1:18.

love of Christ who suffered the most painful death out of love for us, to redeem us from eternal death. Accordingly, St Paul says: "Our life is hidden with Christ in God, but when our life appears, then we shall also appear with him in glory" (Colossians 3:3-4).

Why then should we be afraid to die, considering the many comforting promises of the gospel and of the holy scriptures? "God the Father has given us everlasting life," says St John, "and this life is in his Son. The one who has the Son has life, and the one who does not have the Son does not have life. And I write this," says St John, "to you who believe in the name of the Son of God, so that you may know that you have everlasting life, and that you believe in the name of the Son of God" (1 John 5:11-13). And our Saviour Christ says, "The one who believes in me has everlasting life, and I will raise them from death to life on the last day" (John 6:40, 47). St Paul also says that "Christ has become for us our righteousness, our holiness, and redemption from God, so let the one who boasts, boast in the Lord" (1 Corinthians 1:30-31). St Paul set little store by all other things and treated them with contempt, considering the things which cost him dearly before as like dung, that he might be found in Christ and have everlasting life, true holiness, righteousness, and redemption (Philippians 3:7-11).

Finally, St Paul makes a plain argument in this way: "If our heavenly Father would not spare his own natural Son, but gave him up to death for us, how can it be that, with him, he should not give us all things?" (Romans 8:32). Therefore, if we have Christ, then we have with him and by him all good things, whatever we wish or desire in our hearts, such as victory over death, sin, and hell. We have the favour of God, peace with him, holiness, wisdom, justice, power, life, and redemption. We have, by him, perpetual health, wealth, joy, and everlasting bliss.

THE GAINS AND PAINS OF DEATH

So far it has been shown to you that there are three reasons why people commonly fear death. First, the sorrowful departing from worldly goods and pleasures; second, the fear of the pangs and pains that come with death; and finally the principal cause is the horrible fear of extreme misery and perpetual damnation in time to come. And yet none of these three reasons trouble good people, because they reassure themselves by true faith, perfect love, and the sure hope of endless joy and everlasting bliss.

THE GAINS OF DEATH

Therefore, all those who are joined to Christ with true faith, steadfast hope, and perfect love have great cause to be full of joy, and not to fear death or everlasting damnation. For death cannot deprive them of Jesus Christ, and no sin can condemn them (Romans 8:1). They are are safely grafted into him who is their only joy, treasure, and life. Let us repent of our sins, amend our lives, trust in his mercy and satisfaction, and death can neither take him from us, nor us from him. For as St Paul says, "Whether we live or die, we are the Lord's." And again he says, "Christ died and rose again so that he might be Lord of both the dead and the living" (Romans 14:8-9). So if we are the Lord's, when we are dead, it must therefore follow that such temporal death cannot harm us, but also that it will be much to our profit and join us to God more perfectly.

The Christian heart may surely be convinced of this by the infallible truth of holy scripture. God has prepared us for immortality, says St Paul, and given us the Spirit as a deposit guaranteeing what is to come (2 Corinthians 5:5). Therefore, let us always be confident, for we know that as long as we are in the body we are (as it were) far from God in a foreign country, subject to many perils, walking without perfect sight and knowledge of Almighty God, only seeing him by faith in the holy scriptures. But we have courage and a desire to be at home with God and our saviour Christ, far from the body (2 Corinthians 5:6-8), where we may behold his godhead, as he is, face to face, to our everlasting comfort (1 John 3:2; 1 Corinthians 13:12). These are, in effect, St Paul's words, by which we may perceive that life in this world is compared to a pilgrimage in a foreign country far from God. And we see that death, delivering us from our bodies, sends us straight home to our own country, and makes us dwell in the presence of God for ever, in perpetual rest and quietness. So to die is no loss, but profit and winning, for all true Christian people (Philippians 1:21).

What did the thief who hung on a cross with Christ lose by his bodily death? Indeed, how much did he gain by it? Did not our saviour say to him, "Today you shall be with me in Paradise" (Luke 23:43)? And Lazarus, that pitiable person who lay at the rich man's gate afflicted with sores and pining with hunger: did not death highly profit and promote him? By the ministry of angels he was sent to Abraham's side, a place of rest, joy, and heavenly consolation (Luke 16:20-22). Let us not think otherwise (good Christian people) than that Christ has prepared the same joy and happiness for us, which he prepared for Lazarus and the thief. Therefore, let us stick to his salvation and gracious redemption, and believe his word, serve him from our hearts, and obey him. And whatever we have done before which is contrary to his most holy will, let us repent of it now, and in future be careful to correct our life. And we will undoubtedly find him as merciful to us as he was to both Lazarus and the thief. Their examples are written in holy scripture for the comfort of those who are sinners and subject to sorrows, miseries, and calamities in this world, that they should not despair of God's mercy but always trust to have forgiveness of their sins by it, and everlasting life, as Lazarus and the thief had.

So, I trust every Christian perceives by the infallible word of God that bodily death cannot harm or hinder those who truly believe in Christ. On the contrary, it shall profit and promote Christian souls who, being truly penitent for their offences, depart in perfect love and in sure trust that God is merciful to them, forgiving their sins for the merits of Jesus Christ, his only natural Son.

PAIN BEFORE GAIN

The second reason why some fear death is the terrible sickness and grievous pains which partly come before death, and partly accompany death whenever it comes. This fear is the fear of our frail flesh, and a natural emotion belonging to the nature of a mortal person. But true faith in God's promises, and a regard for the pains and pangs which Christ suffered on the cross for us pitiable sinners, with a consideration of the joy and everlasting life to come in heaven, will lessen those pains and moderate this fear. So it shall never be able to overthrow the hearty desire and gladness that the Christian soul has to be separated from this corrupt body so that it may come to the gracious presence of our saviour Jesus Christ.

If we steadfastly believe the word of God, we shall perceive that such bodily sickness, pangs of death, or whatever distressing pains we suffer whether before or with death, are nothing else for Christians but the discipline of our heavenly and loving Father. With this discipline, he mercifully corrects us, to test and declare the faith of his patient children that they may be found praiseworthy, glorious, and honourable in his sight when Jesus Christ shall be openly revealed as judge of all the world; or else he chastises us to amend in us whatever offends his fatherly and gracious goodness, so that we should not perish everlastingly. And this correcting discipline is common to all those who are truly his.

Therefore, let us cast away the burden of sin that lies so heavily on our necks, and return to God by true repentance and amendment of our lives. Let us with patience run this race that is appointed, suffering for the sake of him who died for our salvation all the sorrows and pangs of death, and death itself joyfully, when God sends it to us, having our eyes always fixed on the head and captain of our faith, Jesus Christ. For the joy that was set before him, he cared neither for the shame or pain of death, but willingly conformed his will to his Father's will, most patiently suffering the most shameful and painful death of the cross, even though he was innocent (Hebrews 12:1-2). And now, therefore, he is exalted in heaven and sits forever on the right hand of the throne of God the Father (Philippians 2:9).

Let us remember, therefore, the life and joys of heaven which are kept for all of those who patiently suffer here with Christ. And let us consider that Christ suffered all these pains at the hands of sinners, and for sinners, and then we shall with patience more easily suffer such sorrows and pains when they come. Let us not make light of the discipline of the Lord, nor hold a grudge against him or fall away from him when we are corrected by him. For the Lord loves those whom he corrects and chastens everyone he accepts as his child. What child is there whom the Father loves, says St Paul, whom he does not also chastise? If you are not corrected by God (which all his well beloved and true children are) then you are not truly recognised by God as his children. Therefore, seeing as when we have human fathers here on earth we respect them and reverently submit to their correction, how much more should we be in subjection to our spiritual Father, from whom we shall have eternal life? Our human fathers may sometimes correct us as seems best to them, without cause. But this Father justly corrects us, either for our sin so that we can change, or for our benefit and good, to make us by this partakers of his holiness. Furthermore, all the correction which God sends us in this present time seems to have no joy and comfort, but only sorrow and pain; yet it brings with it a taste of God's mercy and goodness towards those who are thus corrected, and a sure hope of God's everlasting consolation in heaven (Hebrews 12:5-11).

These sorrows, diseases, and sicknesses, and also death itself, are nothing else but our heavenly Father's discipline. By these he assures us of his love and gracious favour. By these he tests and purifies us. And by these he gives to us holiness and assures us that we are his children and he is our merciful Father. And so should we not then, with all humility, as obedient and loving children, joyfully embrace this discipline and always say in our heart, with our saviour Jesus Christ: Father, if this anguish and sorrow which

I feel, and death which I see approaching, may not pass, but your will is that I must suffer them, then may your will be done (Matthew 26:42).

The Christian's Reward

In this sermon against the fear of death, two reasons have been given which commonly move worldly people to be very afraid to die. And yet those reasons do not trouble the faithful who live well, when death comes, but rather give them an opportunity greatly to rejoice, considering that they shall be delivered from the sorrow and misery of this world and be brought to the great joy and happiness of the life to come.

Blessed immortality

Now, the third and special cause why death is indeed to be feared is the miserable state of worldly and ungodly people after their death. But this is no reason at all why godly and faithful people should fear death, but rather the opposite: their godly way of living in this life, and their belief in Christ, clinging continually to his merits, should make them long greatly for that life which undoubtedly waits for them after this bodily death. There are many plain places of scripture about this immortal state after this transitory life where we shall live forever in the presence of God in joy and rest after victory over all sickness, sorrows, sin, and death. These places confirm the weak conscience against the fear of all such distress, sickness, sin, and bodily death, to relieve such trembling and ungodly fear, and to encourage us with the comfort and hope of a blessed state after this life.

St Paul wished for the Ephesians that "God, the Father of glory would give to them the spirit of wisdom and revelation, that the eyes of their hearts might have light to know him", and to perceive what great things he had called them to, and how rich is the inheritance he has prepared after this life for those who belong to him (Ephesians 1:17-18). And St Paul himself declared the desire of his heart, which was to be freed from his body and to be with Christ which, as he said, was much better for him, although to them it was more necessary that he should live, which he did not deny for their sakes (Philippians 1:23-26). Just as St Martin said, "Good Lord, if I am still necessary for your people, to do good to them, I will refuse no labour. But otherwise, for my own self, I plead with you to take my soul."[3]

Now, the holy fathers of the old law, and all the faithful and righteous people who died before our saviour Christ's ascension into heaven, by death departed from troubles to rest, from the hands of their enemies into the hands of God, from sorrows and sicknesses to joyful refreshing at Abraham's side, a place of comfort and consolation as the scriptures plainly testify. And the book of Wisdom says that "the souls of the righteous are in the hand of God, and no torment shall touch them. They seemed to the eyes of the foolish to die, and their death was counted miserable, and their departing out of this world as wretched. But they are in rest."[4] And another place says, "the righteous shall live forever, and their reward is with the Lord, and their minds are with God who is above all. Therefore, they shall receive a glorious kingdom and a beautiful crown at the Lord's hand."[5] And in another place in the same book it says, "even if the righteous die prematurely, they will be at rest", where they shall be refreshed.[6] Concerning Abraham's side, Christ's words are so plain that a Christian needs no more proof of it (Luke 16:22-26).

---

3   Martin (316-397) was Bishop of Tours in France but was born in what is now Hungary. This quote concerning his death comes from Sulpicius Severus (363-425), a Christian writer from Aquitaine in France, who wrote to his mother-in-law about Martin's death. See his *Epistola 3, ad Bassulam* (PL 20:182; NPNF[2] 11:22).

4   From the apocryphal book of The Wisdom of Solomon 3:1-3.

5   Wisdom 5:15-16.

6   Wisdom 4:7.

To be with Christ

Now then, if this is the state of the holy fathers and righteous people before the coming of our saviour, and before he was glorified, how much more then ought we all to have a steadfast faith and a sure hope of this blessed state and condition after our death? Our saviour has now performed the whole work of our redemption and is gloriously ascended into heaven to prepare our dwelling places with him (John 14:2). He said to his Father, "I want my servants to be with me where I am" (John 12:26, 17:24). And we know that whatever Christ wants, his Father wants the same, so it must be that if we are his faithful servants, our souls will be with him after we depart out of this present life.

Even in the midst of his torments as he was stoned to death, what was St Stephen's mind thinking about above all? "When he was full of the Holy Spirit," says holy scripture, "he lifted up his eyes to heaven and saw the glory of God, and Jesus standing at the right hand of God." After he had confessed this boldly before the enemies of Christ, they dragged him out of the city and there they stoned him. And he cried out to God saying, "Lord Jesus Christ, receive my spirit" (Acts 7:55-59). And does not our saviour say plainly in John's Gospel, "Truly truly I say to you, the one who hears my word and believes in him who sent me has everlasting life and will not come into judgment but passes into life" (John 5:24)? Should we not then think of that death as precious, by which we pass into life? Therefore, it is a true saying of the prophet: "the death of holy and righteous people is precious in the Lord's sight" (Psalm 116:15). Holy Simeon, after he had his heart's desire and saw our saviour for whom he longed his whole life, embraced him in his arms and said, "Now Lord, let me depart in peace, for my eyes have seen the salvation which you have prepared for all nations" (Luke 2:28-31).

It is true, therefore, that the death of the righteous is called peace and a benefit from God, as the Church says in the name of the righteous departed out of this world, "My soul, turn to your rest for the Lord has been good to you and rewarded you" (Psalm 116:7).[7] As we see from holy scripture and other ancient histories of the martyrs, ever since Christ's ascension the holy, faithful, and righteous have not doubted that in their death they were going in spirit to be with Christ, who is our life, health, wealth, and salvation.

In his holy Revelation, John saw one hundred and forty-four thousand virgins and innocents, of whom he said, "These follow the Lamb, Jesus Christ, wherever he goes" (Revelation 14:1-5). And shortly afterwards, in the same chapter, he says "I heard a voice from heaven saying to me 'Write this: happy and blessed are the dead who die in the Lord from now on.' Surely, says the Spirit, they shall rest from their pains and labours, for their works will follow them" (Revelation 14:13). So then they shall reap with joy and comfort that which they sowed with labours and pains. "Those who sow to the Spirit, from the Spirit shall reap everlasting life. Let us therefore never be weary of doing good, for when the time of reaping or reward comes, we shall reap everlasting joy without any weariness" (Galatians 6:8-10). Therefore, while we have time (as St Paul exhorts us) let us do good to all people (Galatians 6:10), and not "lay up treasures on earth where rust and moths corrupt it (Matthew 6:19). This rust (as St James says) shall, on the great day, bear witness against us, condemn us, and torment our flesh like a burning fire (James 5:3).

CONSIDER THE FUTURE

Let us beware, therefore, as we steward our own wealth, that we are not in the number of those miserable covetous people whom St James bids to mourn and lament for their greedy accumulation and ungodly keeping of wealth (James 5:1-3). Let us be wise in our use of time, and learn to follow the wise example of the wicked steward in Jesus's parable (Luke 16:1-9). Let us so prudently stew-

---

7   Psalm 116 was recited around the time of burial as part of the 1549 funeral service.

ard our goods and possessions, committed to us here by God for a season, that we may truly hear and obey this commandment of our saviour Christ's: "I say to you, 'Use your worldly wicked wealth to gain friends for yourselves, so that they may receive you into eternal dwellings'" (Luke 16:9). He calls riches "wicked" because the world abuses them for wicked purposes, though they are otherwise a good gift from God and instruments by which God's servants truly serve him in their use of them. He did not command them to make rich friends, to get high dignities and worldly possessions, and to give great gifts to rich people who have no need of them, but to make friends of the poor and pitiable. Whatever they give to those people, Christ accepts it as if given to him. And to these friends, Christ in the Gospel gives such great honour and preeminence, that he says they shall be received into everlasting dwellings. Not that people shall reward us for our good works, but that Christ will reward us and take whatever is done to such friends as if it was done to him.

Making poor wretches our friends like this, we make our saviour Christ our friend, whose members they are. Their misery he takes for his own misery, and their relief, comfort, and help he takes for his own comfort, relief, and help. He will as much thank us and reward us for our goodness shown to them, as if he himself had received the benefit at our hands, as he witnesses in the Gospel saying, "Whatever you have done to any of these simple people who believe in me, you have done that to me" (Matthew 10:42, 18:5, 25:40).

Therefore, let us be diligent that our faith and hope in Almighty God and in our saviour Christ does not fluctuate and fade, and that the love which we pretend to have for him does not turn cold. But let us be careful daily and diligently to show ourselves to be true lovers of God who honour him by keeping his commandments and by doing good deeds to our needy neighbours. And let us, by all means at our disposal relieve their poverty with our abundance, their ignorance with our wisdom and learning, and comfort their weakness with our strength and authority. Let us call everyone back from doing evil, by godly counsel and good example, still persevering in doing good as long as we live. And so we shall not need to fear death for any of the three reasons given before, or for any other reason that can be imagined.

But on the contrary, let us consider the manifold sicknesses, troubles, and sorrows of this present life, the dangers of this perilous pilgrimage, and the great burden which our spirit has in this sinful flesh and frail body subject to death. Let us consider also the manifest sorrows and dangerous deceits of this world on every side: the intolerable pride and covetousness and lechery in times of prosperity; the impatient murmuring of those who are worldly in times of adversity, which continually pull us back and pluck us away from God, our saviour Christ, our life, wealth, and eternal joy and salvation. Let us also consider the innumerable assaults of our spiritual enemy the Devil, with all his fiery darts of ambition, pride, lechery, vainglory, envy, malice, backbiting, and his other innumerable deceits, plots, and snares with which he busily tries to capture everyone under his dominion. He is always like a roaring lion, searching for people to devour by any means (1 Peter 5:8).

The faithful Christian considers all these miseries, perils, and inconveniences to which they are subject as long as they live here on earth. They also consider that blessed and comfortable state of the heavenly life to come, and the sweet condition of those who depart in the Lord, how they are delivered from the continual burdens of their mortal and sinful bodies, from all malice, schemes, and deceits of this world and from all the assaults of their spiritual enemy the Devil, to live in peace, rest, and perpetual quietness, to live in the fellowship of innumerable angels, and with the congregation of "the righteous made perfect" such as the patriarchs, prophets, martyrs, and confessors (Hebrews 12:22-23), and finally to come to the presence of Almighty God and our saviour Jesus Christ.

The one who considers all these things and confidently believes them from the bottom of their heart, is established in God, in this true faith, having a quiet conscience in Christ, a firm hope, and an assured trust in God's mercy through the merits of Jesus Christ. They shall obtain this quietness, rest, and eternal joy, and shall be without fear of bodily death when it comes. Like St Paul, they certainly shall (according to God's will and when it pleases God to call them out of this life) gladly and greatly desire in their heart to be rid of all this evil, and live always for God's pleasure in perfect obedience to his will with our saviour Jesus Christ (Philippians 1:23). May the Lord bring us to his gracious presence by his infinite mercy and grace, to reign with him in life everlasting. To him, with our heavenly Father and the Holy Spirit, be glory forever and ever. *Amen.*

HOMILY 10

Obedience to Authorities

Almighty God has created and appointed all things in heaven, on earth, and in the waters, in a most excellent and perfect order. In heaven, he has appointed distinct orders and states of Archangels and Angels. On earth, he has assigned kings and rulers, with other governors under them, all in good and necessary order. The water above is kept and rains down in due time and season. The sun, moon, stars, rainbow, thunder, lightning, clouds, and all the birds of the air keep their order. The earth, trees, seeds, plants, herbs, corn, grass, and all manner of beasts, keep in their order. All the parts of the whole year—winter, summer, months, nights, and days—continue in their order. All kinds of fish in the sea, rivers, and waters, with all fountains, springs, and indeed the seas themselves, keep their beautiful course and order.

Mankind itself also, has all its parts, both within and without—soul, heart, mind, memory, understanding, reason, speech, with each and every physical part of their bodies in a profitable, necessary, and pleasant order. Every kind of person in their vocation, calling, and office, has appointed to them their duty and order. Some are in high positions, some in low; some kings and rulers, some servants and subjects; priests and laypeople; employers and employees; fathers and children; husbands and wives; rich and poor. Every one needs the others, so that in all things the godly order of God is

---

* The original title of this Homily was *An Exhortation, concerning Good Order and Obedience to Rulers and Magistrate*s.

to be applauded and praised, because without it no house, no city, no commonwealth, can continue and endure. For where there is no right order, there reigns all abuse, carnal liberty, crime, sin, and confusion like at Babel (Genesis 11:1-9).

Godly order

Take away kings, rulers, magistrates, judges, and such divinely-ordained roles, and no one could travel or move about without being robbed, or sleep in their own house or bed without being murdered. No one could keep their spouse, children, or possessions safe. All things would be common and there would necessarily follow all mischief and utter destruction, both of souls, bodies, goods, and commonwealths.[1] Blessed be God that we in this realm of England do not feel the horrible calamities, miseries, and wretchedness which all those who lack this godly order do undoubtedly feel and suffer. And praise God that we know the great and excellent benefit of God shown towards us in this manner. God has sent us his high gift, our most dear sovereign Lord, King Edward the Sixth, with godly, wise, and honourable counsel, with other governors and servants in a beautiful order.

Therefore, let us subjects do our bounden duties, giving hearty thanks to God and praying for the preservation of this godly order. Let us all obey, even from the bottom of our hearts, all their godly proceedings, laws, statutes, proclamations, and injunctions, with all other godly orders. Let us consider the scriptures of the Holy Spirit, which persuade and command us all to be obedient. First and chiefly, we must be subject to the King's Majesty, supreme head over all; and next, to his honourable government, and to all other authorities, magistrates, and officers who by God's goodness are appointed and ordered. For

---

1 Shakespeare may recall these paragraphs, in *Troilus and Cressida*, Act 1 Scene 3, in a speech of Ulysses where he says of good order, "untune that string, And hark what discord follows!" Cf. Pseudo-Demosthenes, *Oration against Aristogeiton* (LCL 299: 523-531): "every law is an invention and gift of the gods", and without obedience to the laws made by the rulers, "all is dissolved, broken up, confounded, and the city becomes the prey of the most profligate and shameless."

Almighty God is the only author and provider of this state and order, as it is written by God in the book of the Proverbs, "By me kings rule, and rulers decree what is right; by me princes govern, and nobles—all who reign on earth. I love those who love me, and those who seek for me, find me" (Proverbs 8:15-17).

Here let us mark well and remember that the high power and authority of rulers, with the making of laws, judgments, and officers, are the ordinances not of people, but of God. That is why I repeat this point so many times. Here it is also to be considered and remembered that this good order is appointed by God's wisdom, favour, and love, especially for those who love God, and therefore he says, "I love those who love me" (Proverbs 8:17). Also, in the book of Wisdom, we may evidently learn that a ruler's power, authority, and strength is a great benefit of God, given by his great mercy for the comfort of our misery. For thus we read there, it is said to rulers: "Hear O kings, and understand. You who are judges of the ends of the earth, learn. Give ear, you who rule the multitudes, for your power is given to you by the Lord, and your strength comes from the Most High."[2] Let us also learn here from the infallible word of God that kings and other supreme and high office holders are ordained by God, who is the highest, and therefore they are diligently taught to apply themselves to knowledge and wisdom, necessary for the right ordering of God's people committed to their governance. They are here also taught by Almighty God that they should acknowledge themselves to have all their power and strength not from Rome, but immediately from God Most High.[3]

---

2   From the apocryphal book of Wisdom 6:1-3.

3   This is perhaps the closest the Homilies come to suggesting that the apocryphal book, the Wisdom of Solomon, is part of infallible scripture. Article 5 of the *Forty-two Articles* (1553) would later rule out the use of the Apocrypha (including Wisdom) for establishing doctrine (cf. Article 6 of the *Thirty-nine Articles* in 1571), but such books could still be read "for example of life and instruction of manners". Either way, however, Wisdom here simply repeats the point just made from the canonical book of Proverbs, and since the Roman Church accepted Wisdom as part of scripture, the Homily's use of this against any papal claim to universal jurisdiction retains a certain rhetorical force.

OBEY THE AUTHORITIES

We read in the book of Deuteronomy that all punishment belongs to God, in this sentence: "vengeance is mine, and I will repay" (Deuteronomy 32:35).[4] But we must understand this sentence to apply also to the magistrates who stand in God's place in judgment and punishment, by good and godly laws, here on earth. The places of scripture which seem to remove judgment, punishment, or killing from Christians, ought to be understood in this way: that no one, of their own private authority, may be judge over others to punish or kill. But we must refer all judgment to God, to kings and rulers, and judges under them, who are God's officers to execute justice. And by the plain words of scripture they have their authority, and the use of the sword granted by God, as we are taught by St Paul, the dear and elect apostle of our saviour Christ, whom we ought diligently to obey even as we would obey our saviour Christ if he were present. Thus St Paul writes to the Romans:

> "Let everyone be submissive to the governing authorities. For there is no authority except that which God has established. The authorities that we have are established by God. Therefore, whoever rebels against such authority is resisting what God has instituted. Those who do so, will bring judgment on themselves. For rulers hold no terror for those who do what is right, but for those who do what is wrong. Do you want to be free from fear of the one who is in authority? Then do what is right and you will be praised. For the one in authority is God's servant, to do you good. But if you do what is wrong, be afraid, for rulers do not bear the sword for nothing. They are God's servants, to avenge and bring punishment on the wrongdoer. Therefore, it is necessary to submit to the authorities, not only in order to avoid such punishment, but also as a matter of conscience. This is also why you pay taxes, for the authorities are God's servants, who give their time and attention to governing" (Romans 13:1-6).

Here let us all learn from St Paul, the chosen instrument of God

---

4   See also Romans 12:19 and Hebrews 10:30.

(Acts 9:15), that all people having souls owe a duty, even in conscience, obedience, submission, and subjection to the high powers which are constituted in authority by God. He excepts none, exempts none, neither priest, apostle, nor prophet, as Chrysostom points out.[5] For they are God's lieutenants, God's presidents, God's officers, God's commissioners, God's judges ordained by God himself, from whom alone they have all their power and all their authority. And the same St Paul threatens nothing less than everlasting damnation to all disobedient people, to all those who resist this general and common authority. For they resist not people, but God; not a human design or invention, but God's wisdom, God's order, power, and authority.

Rebellion Prohibited

Since God has created and arranged all things in a beautiful order, we have been taught in the first part of this sermon concerning good order and obedience that we also ought in all commonwealths to observe and keep a due order, and to be obedient to the authorities, their ordinances and laws. We have been taught that all rulers are appointed by God so that a godly order is kept in the world, and also how magistrates ought to learn how to rule and govern according to God's laws. We have also been taught that all subjects are bound to obey them as God's servants, even if they are evil, not only out of fear but also for the sake of conscience.

Resisting the Authorities

And now, good people, let us all be diligent to note that it is not lawful for servants and subjects ever to resist or stand against the superior powers. For St Paul's words are plain, that "whoever rebels will bring judgment on themselves", because, "whoever rebels is rebelling against what God has instituted" (Romans 13:2). Our saviour Christ himself, and his apostles, received many and vari-

---

5   See Chrysostom's Homily 23 on Romans 13:1 (PG 60:615; NPNF 11:511).

149

ous injuries from unfaithful and wicked people in authority; yet we never read that any of them caused any sedition or rebellion against authority. We often read that they patiently suffered all troubles, vexations, slanders, pangs, and pains, and death itself obediently, without disorder or resistance. They committed their cause to him who judges righteously (1 Peter 2:23), and prayed for their enemies heartily and earnestly. They knew that the authority of the powers that be was God's ordinance, and therefore both in their words and deeds they always taught obedience to it, and never taught or did the opposite.

The wicked judge, Pontius Pilate said to Christ, "Do you not realise that I have the power either to free you or to crucify you?" And Jesus answered, "You would have no power at all against me if it were not given to you from above" (John 19:10-11). Christ taught us plainly by this that even wicked rulers have their power and authority from God. And therefore it is not lawful for their subjects to resist them by force, even if they abuse their power. Far less is it lawful for subjects to resist their godly and Christian rulers who do not abuse their authority but use it to God's glory and to the profit and advantage of God's people.

The holy apostle St Peter commands servants to be obedient to their masters, not only if they are good and gentle but also if they are evil and difficult (1 Peter 2:18-21). He affirms that the mission and calling of God's people is to be patient and endure suffering. And there he points to the patience of our saviour Christ, to persuade us to be obedient to governors, even if they are wicked wrongdoers. But now, let us hear St Peter himself speak, for his own words will best assure our consciences. This is what he says in his first epistle:

> "Servants, submit yourselves to your masters, in reverent fear of God, not only to those who are good and gentle, but also to those who are harsh. For it is commendable if someone endures the pain of unjust suffering because they are mindful of God. But how is it to your credit if you receive a beating for doing wrong, and endure

that? But if you suffer for doing good, and you endure it, this is commendable before God. For this is what you were called to, because Christ suffered for you, leaving you an example, so you might follow in his footsteps" (1 Peter 2:18-21).

All these are the very words of St Peter.

KING DAVID'S EXAMPLE

St David also teaches us a good lesson on this subject. He was many times most cruelly and wrongfully persecuted by King Saul, and many times put in jeopardy and in danger of his life by King Saul and his people. Yet he never resisted, nor did he use any force or violence against King Saul, his mortal enemy, but always served his superior, his Lord and master King Saul, and gave him most true, most diligent, and most faithful service (1 Samuel 18-20). Even when the Lord God had given King Saul into David's hands in his own cave, he would not hurt him, even though he could have easily slain him without danger to himself. No, he would not allow any of his servants to even lay their hands on King Saul, but prayed to God in this way: "The LORD forbid that I should do such a thing to my Master, the LORD's anointed, or lay my hands on him; for he is the LORD's anointed" (1 Samuel 24:6). That David might have killed his enemy, King Saul, is clearly proven in 1 Samuel, both by David's cutting off the corner of Saul's robe (1 Samuel 24:4) and by the plain confession of King Saul (1 Samuel 24:18-19).

Another time, mentioned in the same book, the most unmerciful and unkind King Saul persecuted poor David. And God gave King Saul into David's hands by putting King Saul and his whole army into a deep sleep. David, and Abishai with him, went in the night into Saul's camp, where Saul lay sleeping with his spear stuck in the ground near his head. Abishai said to David, "God has delivered your enemy into your hands today. Now, therefore, let me pin him to the ground with one thrust of my spear, and I will not strike him a second time"—meaning by this to kill him with one stroke and be done with him forever. But David answered and said to Abishai, "Do not destroy him. For who can lay his hands on the LORD's anointed and be guiltless?" And David added, "as surely as the LORD lives, the LORD shall strike him, or his day to die shall come, or he shall go down into battle and perish there. The LORD keep me from laying my hands on the LORD's anointed. But take the spear that is at his head and the jug of water, and let us go." And so he did (1 Samuel 26:7-12). Here it is evidently proven that we may not resist, nor in any way hurt an anointed king, who is God's lieutenant, deputy, and highest servant in that country where he is king.

But perhaps some here would say that David might have killed King Saul in his own defence, lawfully and with a safe conscience. But holy David knew that he should in no way resist, hurt, or kill his sovereign Lord and King. He knew that he was but King Saul's subject, even though he was in great favour with God and his enemy King Saul was out of God's favour. Therefore, even though he was greatly provoked, he utterly refused to hurt the LORD's anointed. For fear of offending God and his own conscience, he did not dare even once to lay his hands on God's high officer, the king, even though he had occasion and opportunity, and he knew the king was under God's punishment and judgment and kept safe only for the sake of his office. Therefore he prayed so often and so earnestly that he might not lay his hands on the LORD's anointed.

St David is named in scripture as "a man after God's own heart" (1 Samuel 13:14 and Acts 13:22). By these two examples he gives a general rule and lesson to all subjects in the world, not to resist their sovereign Lord and ruler, and not to take up a sword by their private authority against their ruler, God's anointed, who only bears the sword by God's authority for the maintenance of good and the punishment of evil. By God's law and commandment, rulers have the use of the sword and all power, jurisdiction, rule, and coercive force as supreme governor of all their realms and dominions by the authority of God and by God's ordinances.

Another notable story which also teaches this doctrine is found in 2 Samuel. When an Amalekite had killed King Saul by King Saul's own consent and commandment, he went to David, supposing that he would be greatly thanked for his message that he had killed David's mortal enemy. He therefore made great haste to tell David what had happened, taking with him King Saul's crown from his head and the bracelet from his arm to persuade him of the truth of his story. But godly David was so far from rejoicing at this news that he immediately tore his clothes from his back, mourned and wept, and said to the messenger, "How is it that you were not afraid to lay hands on the LORD's anointed to destroy him?" And so David made one of his servants kill the messenger, saying, "Your blood be on your own head, for your mouth testified against you when you said 'I killed the LORD's anointed'" (2 Samuel 1:1-16).

Since these examples are so many and so clear, it is intolerable ignorance, madness, and wickedness for subjects to incite any murmuring, rebellion, resistance, commotion, or insurrection against their dear and most revered sovereign Lord and ruler, ordained and appointed by God's goodness for their advantage, peace, and quietness.

OBEY GOD ABOVE ALL

However, let us undoubtedly believe (good Christian people) that we may not obey rulers, magistrates, or any other authority—even our own fathers—if they command us to do anything contrary to God's commandments. In such a case, we ought to say with the apostles, "We must obey God, rather than human beings" (Acts 5:29).

Even in that case, however, we may not in any way violently resist or rebel against rulers, or make any insurrection, sedition, or disorder either by force of arms or otherwise against the anointed of the Lord or any of their appointed officers. But we must in such a case patiently suffer all wrongs and injuries, referring the judgment of our cause only to God.

Let us fear the terrible punishment of Almighty God against

traitors or rebellious people, such as in the case of Korah, Dathan, and Abiram who grumbled and opposed God's magistrates and officers—and therefore the earth opened and swallowed them up alive. Others, for their wicked murmuring and rebellion, were utterly consumed by a sudden fire sent by God (Numbers 11 and 16). Others, for their opposition to their rulers and governors (God's servants) were suddenly stricken with a foul skin disease (Numbers 12:10). Others were stung to death by strange fiery serpents (Numbers 21:6). Others were badly plagued, so that fourteen thousand seven hundred were killed in one day for rebellion against those whom God had appointed to be in authority (Numbers 16:41-49). Absalom also, rebelling against his father, King David, was punished with a strange and notable death (2 Samuel 18:9-15).

PRAYER FOR PROPER AUTHORITIES

So far in this sermon on good order and obedience, you have seen it manifestly proven from the scriptures and examples that all subjects are bound to obey those in authority over them. They are not for any reason to resist, rebel, or plot sedition against them, even if they are wicked. Let no one think that they can escape unpunished if they commit treason, conspiracy, or rebellion against their sovereign ruler, even if they do so secretly in thought, word, or deed ever so privately in their own room by themselves, or openly communicating and consulting with others.

TREASON

For treason will not be hidden. Treason will be exposed in the end. God will both expose and punish that most detestable vice, for it goes directly against his ordinance and against his high principal judge and anointed one on earth. The violence and injury that is committed against authority is committed against God, the commonwealth, and the whole realm. God will have this revealed and rightly punished one way or another. For it is notably written by the wise man in scripture, in the book called Ecclesiastes, "Do not curse the king, even in your thoughts, or curse the rich in your bedroom, because a bird in the air may carry your words, and a bird on the wing may report it" (Ecclesiastes 10:20).

These lessons and examples are written for our learning. Let us all therefore fear the most detestable vice of rebellion, always knowing and remembering that the one who resists common authority resists God and his ordinance, as it may be proven by many other places of holy scripture.

THE POPE'S PRETENCE OF POWER

Here let us take heed that we do not misunderstand these and such places which so directly command obedience to superiors and so straightforwardly punish rebellion and disobedience. They are not meant in any way to apply to the pretended power of the bishop of Rome. For truly the scripture of God allows no such usurped power, full of crimes, abuses, and blasphemies. But the true meaning of these and such places is to praise and declare God's true ordinance, and the authority of God's anointed kings and their officers appointed under them.

Concerning the usurped power of the bishop of Rome, who most wrongly claims to be the successor of Christ and Peter, we may easily perceive how false, fake, and forged it is. It has no sufficient basis in holy scripture, and we may easily see how wrong it is by the fruits and doctrine of it. For our saviour Christ and St Peter both agree in teaching most earnestly our obedience to kings, as the chief and supreme rulers in the world under God. But the Bishop of Rome teaches that those who are under him are free from all the burdens and charges of the commonwealth, and free from obedience to their ruler.[6] This is most clearly against Christ's doctrine and St Peter's. He ought therefore to be called Antichrist, and the successor of the Scribes and Pharisees, rather

---

6   This teaching lies behind the insistence in Article 37 "Of the Civil Magistrate", that, "The Bishop of Rome hath no jurisdiction in this Realm of England."

than Christ's vicar or St Peter's successor.[7] Not only on this point but also on other weighty matters of Christian religion, such as on the cancellation and forgiveness of sins and on salvation, he teaches so directly against both St Peter and against our saviour Christ. They taught obedience to kings and also practised obedience in their daily lives, for we read that that they both paid their taxes (Matthew 17:24-27).

We also read that the holy virgin Mary, mother of our saviour Christ, and Joseph who was believed to be his father, went to the City of David called Bethlehem at the command of the Emperor, to be taxed, as others did. They declared their obedience to the magistrates, for the sake of God's ordinance. And here let us not forget the blessed virgin Mary's obedience. For although she was highly favoured by God, and Christ's natural mother, and was also heavily pregnant at the time and near to giving birth, she still gladly and without any excuse or grudging (for conscience's sake) took that cold and difficult winter journey. And when she gave birth, she even had to place the child in a manger, because there was no guest room available for them (Luke 2:4-7).[8]

St Peter also agrees, writing in these express words in his first letter: "Submit yourselves for the Lord's sake to every human authority: whether to the emperor, as the supreme authority, or to governors, who are sent by him to punish those who do wrong and to commend those who do right. For this is God's will" (1 Peter 2:13-15). I do not need to expound these words, since they are so clear in themselves. St Peter does not say, "Submit your-

---

7   Vicar here means one who stands in someone else's place, acting (vicariously, we might say) as their substitute or deputy (from the Latin, *vicarius*). The designation "Vicar" for a church minister has its origins in a time when a substitute was appointed to look after a parish *in place of* an absent Rector (not an absent God!). Rome does not merely claim with this title that the bishop of Rome *serves* Christ or *ministers* to him, but that he stands in Christ's place, as his substitute or deputy on earth.

8   The Homily originally said that because she was so poor, Mary had to give birth in a stable, but the Gospels do not actually mention a stable or blame the manger on her poverty.

self to me, as supreme head of the Church." Neither does he say, "Submit yourselves in future to my successors in Rome." Rather, he says, "Submit yourselves to your ruler, your supreme head, and those appointed to authority under them." That will demonstrate your obedience. That is the will of God. God wills that you are in subjection to your head and king. That is his ordinance, his commandment, and God's holy will—that the whole body of every realm, and all the members and parts of it, shall be subject to their head, their ruler, and that (as St Peter writes) for the Lord's sake. St Paul adds that it is for conscience's sake too, and not only out of fear (Romans 13:5).

Thus we learn from the word of God to yield to our ruler what is due to them, that is, honour, obedience, payment of due taxes, customs, revenue, fees, love and reverence.

PRAYER FOR OUR RULERS

Thus we see in part what our duty is towards common authority. Now let us learn to live this out. And let us instantly and heartily pray to God, the only author of all authority, for all those who are in positions of authority. As St Paul writes to Timothy: "First of all, then, I urge that petitions, prayers, intercessions and thanksgivings be made for all people—for kings and all those in positions of authority, so that we may live peaceful and quiet lives which are godly and dignified in every way. This is good, and pleases God our Saviour" (1 Timothy 2:1-3). Here Paul makes an earnest and special exhortation concerning thanksgiving and prayer for kings and rulers, as if to say, above all things you must principally and chiefly pray for rulers.

Let us heartily thank God for his great and excellent goodness and providence to us in this regard. Let us pray for our rulers, that they may have God's favour and God's protection. Let us pray that they may always in all things have God before their eyes. Let us pray that they may have wisdom, strength, justice, mercy, zeal for God's glory and his truth, and for Christian souls and the commonwealth. Let us pray that they may rightly use their power and authority for the maintenance and defence of the catholic faith contained in holy scripture.[9] Let us pray that they exercise it both for the benefit of their good and honest subjects, and as agents of wrath to bring punishment on wrongdoers (Romans 13:4).

Let us pray that they may faithfully follow the most faithful kings and captains in the Bible: David, Hezekiah, Josiah, Moses, and others. And let us pray for ourselves, that we may live godly, holy, and Christian lives, and therefore have God on our side (see Psalm 118:6; Hebrews 13:6).[10] And then let us not fear what people can do to us (Psalm 56:11). So we shall live in true obedience, both to our most merciful king in heaven, and to our most Christian king on earth.[11] So we shall please God, and have great benefits, peace of conscience, rest, and quietness here in this world; and after this life, we shall enjoy a better life, rest, peace, and the eternal bliss of heaven. May he who was obedient for us all, even to the death of the cross (Philippians 2:8), grant this to us all—Jesus Christ, to whom with the Father and the Holy Spirit, be all honour and glory, now and forever, *Amen.*

---

9   It needs hardly to be said that this does not mean the Roman Catholic faith, but the "universal" faith of the scriptures and the generally agreed creeds (from the Latin and Greek term, *catholicus*, καθολικός meaning universal or general).

10 The 1547 edition cites the apocryphal book of Judith 5:17, "And as long as they did not sin in the sight of their God, good fortune was with them, for with them is a God who hates injustice." (NETS)

11 i.e. King Edward VI (reigned 1547-1553).

HOMILY 11

ADULTERY AND SEXUAL SIN

G ood Christian people, there is no lack of great swarms of vices which are worthy to be rebuked (into such decay has true godliness and virtuous living now come). Yet above other vices, the outrageous sea of adultery, promiscuity, fornication,[1] and uncleanness has not only burst in, but also overwhelmed almost the whole world. This is to the great dishonour of God, a great disgrace to the name of Christ, the notable decay of true religion, and the utter destruction of the public wealth.

This vice is so abundantly common and has grown to such a height that among many it is counted no sin at all, but rather a pastime, a dalliance, and but a touch of youth—not rebuked but winked at, not punished but laughed at. Therefore it is necessary at this present time to implore you about the sin of promiscuity and fornication, declaring to you the greatness of this sin, and how odious, hateful, and abominable it is and has always been considered by God and all good people; and how grievously it has been punished, both by the law of God, and the laws of various countries. Also, it is necessary to show you certain remedies, by which you may (through the grace of God) avoid this most detest-

---

1   Literally, whoredom and fornication. The former could refer to prostitution or promiscuity / sexual sin in general, and the latter is a catch-all term for sex outside of heterosexual marriage.

*   The original title of this Homily was *An Homily of Whoredom and Uncleanness*.

able sin of promiscuity and fornication, and lead your lives in all honesty and cleanness.

JESUS'S TEACHING

If you call to mind this commandment of God—"You shall not commit adultery"—you will perceive that fornication and promiscuity are most abominable sins in the sight of God. The word "adultery" properly means the unlawful joining together of a married man with any woman except his wife, or of a wife with any man except her husband. Yet it also signifies all unlawful use of those body parts which are set apart for procreation. And this one commandment forbidding adultery, sufficiently paints the picture before our eyes of the greatness of this sin of sexual immorality, and clearly declares how greatly it should be abhorred by all honest and faithful people. None of us should think of themselves as excepted from this commandment, whether we are old or young, married or unmarried, man or woman. Hear what God the Father says by his most excellent prophet Moses: "there shall be no prostitute among the daughters of Israel or the sons of Israel" (Deuteronomy 23:17). Here, promiscuity, fornication, and all uncleanness is forbidden, to all kinds of people, all degrees and all ages, without exception.

We should not doubt that this commandment applies to us. For hear what Christ, the perfect teacher of all truth, says in the New Testament. "You have heard", says Christ, "that it was said, 'You shall not commit adultery.' But I say to you that everyone who looks at a woman with lustful intent has already committed adultery with her in his heart" (Matthew 5:27-28). Here our saviour Christ not only confirms and establishes the law against adultery given in the Old Testament by God the Father through his servant Moses, and applies it at full strength, so that it should continually remain for those who profess his name under the new law. He also condemns the gross interpretation of the Scribes and Pharisees, which taught that this commandment only required people to abstain from outward adultery and not from filthy desires and impure lusts. And he teaches us an exact and full perfection of purity and cleanness of life, that we should keep our bodies undefiled, and also keep our hearts pure and free from all evil thoughts, carnal desires, and fleshly inclinations.

How then can we be free from this commandment, in which so great a charge is laid upon us? May a servant do their own will in anything, when they have a commandment from their master to the contrary? Is not Christ our Master? Are not we his servants? How then may we neglect our Master's will and pleasure, and follow our own will and fantasy? "You are my friends," says Christ, "if you do what I command" (John 15:14). Now Christ our Master has commanded us that we should forsake all uncleanness and lechery, both in body and spirit. This therefore we must do, if we seek to please God.

In the Gospel of St Matthew, we read that the Scribes and Pharisees were grievously offended with Christ because his disciples did not keep the traditions of their forefathers. For they did not ceremonially wash their hands when they went to dinner or supper, among other things. Christ answered and said, "Hear and understand: it is not that which enters into the mouth which defiles a person, but that which comes out of the mouth which defiles someone. For those things which proceed out of the mouth comes forth from the heart, and they defile the person. For out of the heart come evil thoughts, murder, adultery, sexual immorality, theft, false witness, blasphemy. These are the things which defile a person" (Matthew 15:1-20). Here we may see that not only murder, theft, false witness, and blasphemy defile someone; but also evil thoughts, adultery, fornication, and sexual immorality.

Therefore, who is so stupid that they will consider sexual immorality and fornication to be things of small importance and of no weight before God? Christ, who is the Truth and cannot lie (John 14:6; Titus 1:2), says that evil thoughts, adultery, sexual immorality, and fornication defile a person. That is to say, they corrupt both the body and the soul, and make the temples of the Holy Spirit into a filthy dunghill or dungeon of unclean spirits;

they make the mansion of God into the dwelling place of Satan.

Again, in the Gospel of John, when the woman caught in adultery was brought to Christ did he not say to her, "Go on your way, and sin no more" (John 8:11)? Does he not here call sexual immorality a sin? And what is the reward of sin, but everlasting death (Romans 6:23)? If sexual immorality is sin, then it is not lawful to commit it. For St John says, "The one who commits sin is of the devil" (1 John 3:8). And our saviour says, "everyone who commits sin is a slave to sin" (John 8:34; Romans 6:16). If sexual immorality was not a sin, surely John the Baptist would never have rebuked King Herod for taking his brother's wife. But he told him plainly that it was not lawful for him to take his brother's wife. He did not wink at the sexual immorality of Herod, even though he was a king of great power, but boldly rebuked him for his wicked and abominable living, even though he lost his head for this (Mark 6:17-29). He would rather suffer death than see God so dishonoured by the breaking of his holy precept, or to suffer sexual immorality to be un-rebuked, even in a king.

If sexual immorality was just a pastime, a dalliance, and a thing of little importance, as many consider it these days, then truly, John was more than twice mad for incurring the displeasure of a king and being cast into prison and losing his head, all for a mere trifle. But John knew very well how filthy, stinking, and abominable the sin of sexual immorality is in the sight of God. And therefore he would not leave it un-rebuked, no, not even in a king. If sexual immorality is not lawful for a king, neither is it lawful for a subject. If it is not lawful in a public official, neither is it lawful in a private person. If it is not lawful in king or subject, in public official or private person, then truly it is not lawful for any man or woman, whoever they are and however old they are.

THE APOSTLES' TEACHING
Furthermore, in the Acts of the Apostles we read that the apostles and elders, with the whole congregation, were gathered together to

encourage the hearts of the faithful in Antioch (who were uneasy because of the false doctrine of certain Jewish preachers). They sent word to the brethren that it seemed good to the Holy Spirit and to them, to charge them with no more than the necessary things. Among other things, therefore they urged them to abstain from idolatry, and fornication. "You will do well to avoid these things," they said (Acts 15:22-29).

Note here how these holy and blessed fathers of Christ's church charged the congregation with nothing more than was necessary. Notice also how fornication and sexual immorality are among those things from which the brethren of Antioch were urged to abstain. It is therefore necessary, by the determination of the Holy Spirit and the apostles and elders, with the whole congregation, that we must abstain from idolatry and superstition and also from fornication and sexual immorality. Is it necessary to salvation to abstain from idolatry? So it is also to abstain from sexual immorality. Is there any better way to lead to damnation than to be an idolator? No, and neither is there a better way to damnation than to be caught up in sexual sin.

Now, where are those people who so lightly esteem the breaking of marriage vows, sexual immorality, fornication, and adultery? It is necessary, says the Holy Spirit, the blessed apostles, the elders, with the whole congregation of Christ—it is necessary to salvation, they say, to abstain from sexual immorality. If it is necessary for salvation, then woe to those who neglect their salvation and give their minds to so filthy and stinking a sin, to so wicked a vice, and to such detestable abomination.

Flee Sexual Immorality!

You have been taught in the first part of this sermon against adultery, how today that vice reigns above all other vices, and what is meant by that word "adultery." You have been taught how holy scripture dissuades us from that filthy sin, and what corruption comes to our souls through the sin of adultery.

PAUL'S TEACHING

Now to continue on this theme, let us hear what the blessed apostle St Paul says on this subject. Writing to the Romans he has these words: "Let us cast aside the deeds of darkness and put on the armour of light. Let us behave properly, as in the daytime, not in wild parties and drunkenness, not in sexual immorality and promiscuity, not in arguments and jealousy. Rather, clothe yourselves with the Lord Jesus Christ, and do not even think about how to satisfy the desires of the flesh" (Romans 13:12-14).

Here the holy apostle urges us to cast away the works of darkness, among which he includes excessive eating and drinking, sexual immorality and debauchery, which all serve this vice and are preparations for the filthy sin of the flesh. He calls them the deeds or works of darkness, not only because they are usually done in darkness or in the night time—"for everyone who does evil hates the light and will not come into the light for fear that their deeds will be exposed" (John 3:20)—but also because they lead the way to that utter darkness "where there shall be weeping and gnashing of teeth" (Matthew 13:42, 50; 22:13; 25:30). Paul says elsewhere in Romans: "Those who are in the flesh cannot please God. We are debtors, but not to the flesh that we should live in accordance with it. For if you live according to the flesh, you will die" (Romans 8:8, 12-13).

Again Paul says: "Flee from sexual immorality. All the other sins a person commits are outside their body, but whoever sins sexually, sins against their own body. Do you not know that your bodies are temples of the Holy Spirit who is in you and whom you have received from God? You are not your own, for you were bought at a price. Therefore glorify God with your bodies" (1 Corinthians 6:18-20). And a little before that he says, "Do you not know that your bodies are members of Christ himself? Shall I then take the members of Christ and unite them with a prostitute? Never! Do you not know that he who unites himself with a prostitute is one with her in body? For it is said, "The two will become one flesh." But whoever is united with the Lord is one with him in spirit" (1 Corinthians 6:15-17).

What godly reasons does the blessed apostle St Paul bring out here to dissuade us from sexual immorality and all uncleanness? Your members, he says, are the temple of the Holy Spirit, and if anyone defiles that temple, God will destroy them (1 Corinthians 3:17). If we are the temple of the Holy Spirit, how unfitting it is then to drive the Holy Spirit from us through sexual sin, and in his place to set the wicked spirits of uncleanness and fornication, and to be joined to them and serve them! "You were bought at a price", he says, "Therefore honour God with your bodies" (1 Corinthians 6:20).

Christ, that innocent Lamb of God, has bought us from the slavery of the devil "not with corruptible gold and silver but with his most precious blood" (1 Peter 1:18-19). Why? That we should fall again into our old uncleanness and abominable living? Surely not! It was so that we should serve him all the days of our lives (Isaiah 38:20), in holiness and righteousness (Luke 1:74-75), and that we should glorify him in our bodies by purity and cleanness of life. He also declares that our bodies are the members of Christ (1 Corinthians 6:15). How unseemly a thing it is then, to cease to be embodied and united with Christ, and through sexual immorality to be joined and made one with a prostitute. What greater dishonour or injury can we do to Christ, than to take away from him the members of his body and to join them with prostitutes, devils, and wicked spirits? And what more dishonour can we do to ourselves than through uncleanness to lose so excellent a dignity and freedom, and to become bondservants and miserable captives to the spirits of darkness?

Let us therefore consider first the glory of Christ and then our state, the dignity and freedom which God has given us by giving us his Holy Spirit. And let us valiantly defend it, against Satan and all his crafty assaults, that Christ may be honoured and that we may not lose our liberty but always remain united in spirit with him.

In the epistle to the Ephesians, the blessed apostle urges that among us "there must not be even a hint of sexual immorality, or of any sort of impurity or greed, because these are inappropriate for God's holy people. Neither should there be obscenity, foolish talking, or coarse joking, which are out of place, but rather there should be thanksgiving. For you can be sure of this: No immoral, impure, or greedy person—that is, an idolater—has any inheritance in the kingdom of Christ and of God" (Ephesians 5:3-5; cf. Galatians 5:19-21 and 1 Corinthians 6:9-10). So that we remember to be holy, pure, and free from all uncleanness, the holy apostle calls us "saints", holy people, because we are sanctified and made holy in the blood of Christ through the Holy Spirit. Now, if we are saints, what have we to do with the lifestyles of unbelievers? St Peter says, "Just as the one who called you is holy, so be holy in all you do; for it is written: 'Be holy, because I am holy'" (1 Peter 1:15-16).

THE EFFECTS OF SEXUAL SIN

So far we have heard how grievous a sin fornication and sexual immorality is, and how greatly God abhors it throughout the whole of scripture. How can it be anything else but a most abominable sin, seeing that it must not even be named among Christians, much less in any way be committed (Ephesians 5:3)? Surely, if we weighed the greatness of this sin and considered it in the right way, we would find the sin of sexual immorality to be that most filthy lake, foul puddle, and stinking sewer into which all kinds of sins and evils flow, and where they have their resting place and home.

For does not the adulterer have a *pride* in their sexual immorality? As the wise man says, "They are glad when they have done evil, and rejoice in the perverseness of evil" (Proverbs 2:14). Is not the sexually immoral person also *idle*, delighting in no godly exercise but only in that most impure and carnal pleasure? Is not their mind also distracted and utterly drawn away from all virtuous studies and fruitful labours, and given only to carnal imaginations? Does not the sexual immoral person give their mind to *gluttony*, so that they are more able to serve their lusts and carnal pleasures? Do they not give their minds to *covetousness* and to dodgy dealing with others so that they are better able to maintain their illicit affairs and continue in their impure and unlawful love? Do they not swell with *envy* against others, fearing that their prey should be allured and taken away from them? And are they not angry and full of *wrath* and displeasure against their own beloveds, if at any time their carnal and devilish requests are turned down?[2]

What sin or kind of sin is it, that is not joined with fornication and sexual immorality? It is a monster of many heads. It receives all kinds of vices and refuses all kinds of virtues. If one individual sin brings damnation, what is to be thought of that sin which is accompanied by all evils and whatever is hateful to God, damnable to mankind, and pleasant to Satan?

Great is the damnation that hangs over the heads of the sexually immoral and adulterers. What else can I say about the other damages which issue and flow out of this stinking puddle of sexual immorality? Is not that treasure, prized above all by honest persons—the good reputation and name of a man or woman—lost through sexual sin? What livelihood, what substance, what goods, what riches, does sexual immorality consume and bring to nothing! What valiantness and strength is many times made weak and destroyed by it! What intelligence is not degraded and defaced through sexual immorality! What beauty, however excellent it might be, is not disfigured through it! Is it not an enemy to the pleasant flower of youth? Does it not bring grey hairs and old age before its time?

What gift of nature, however precious, is not corrupted by sexual sin? Do not sexually transmitted diseases come this way? And where do so many illegitimate children come from, to the high displeasure of God and the dishonour of holy marriage, but from sexual immorality? How many consume all their wealth and possessions, and in the end fall into such extreme poverty that they turn to stealing and are prosecuted, because of this sin! What con-

---

2   The Homily here links sexual immorality (lust) with the other so-called "deadly sins" of pride, sloth, gluttony, greed, envy, and wrath.

tention and even manslaughter comes from sexual sin? How many young women lose their virginity, how many widows are defiled? How much are the public finances impoverished and troubled because of it? How much is God's word regarded with contempt and distorted by sexual sin and those who are sexually immoral?

This vice is the cause of a great number of the divorces which nowadays are so common, to the great displeasure of God and the breaking of the most holy knot and bond of marriage. For when this most detestable sin has once crept into the heart of an adulterer, so that they are entangled with unlawful and unchaste love, straightaway their true and lawful spouse is despised, their presence abhorred, their company hated and avoided, whatever they do is criticised, and there is no peace in the house as long as they are in sight. In short, they must leave because the other can stand them no longer. Thus through sexual immorality the honest and innocent partner is put away and another is put in their place. O abomination!

Christ our saviour, true God and man, coming to restore the law of his heavenly Father to its right sense, understanding, and meaning, among other things reformed the abuse of this law of God (Matthew 19:8-9). For by custom, Jewish men used to divorce their wives at will, for any cause. Christ, correcting this evil custom, taught that if anyone divorced his wife and married another for any reason except adultery (which was then punishable by death), then they were an adulterer, and they also forced their divorced wife to commit adultery if she was joined to any other man (and that man also, joining with her, also committed adultery). What is the state then of those adulterers who for the love of someone other than their spouse put away their true and lawful partner against all law, right, reason, and conscience? Damnable is the state in which they stand. Swift destruction shall fall on them if they do not repent and amend this. For God will not ever suffer holy marriage to be dishonoured, hated, and despised like this. He will decisively punish this carnal and licentious way of living, and cause his holy ordinance to be held in reverence and honour. For surely marriage (as the apostle says) is "honourable among all, and the marriage bed undefiled, but the sexually immoral and fornicators God will judge" (Hebrews 13:4), that is to say, punish and condemn.

Why have we made such an effort to describe and set forth the greatness of the sin of sexual immorality and the damage that comes out of and flows from it? Words will soon fail anyone who tries to set it out according to the full seriousness and heinousness of it. However, this is all spoken with the intent that everyone should flee sexual immorality and live in the fear of God. God grant that it may not be spoken in vain!

The Punishment of Sexual Immorality

In the second part of this sermon against adultery, you have learned how earnestly the scripture warns us to avoid the sin of adultery and to embrace cleanness of life. We saw that through adultery we fall into all kinds of sins and are made bondservants of the devil, but through cleanness of life we live as members of Christ. And finally, we heard how far adultery takes someone from goodness and drives them headlong into all vices, mischief, and misery. Now I will declare to you next with what grievous punishments God in times past plagued adultery, and how certain secular rulers also punished it. By this you will perceive that sexual immorality and fornication are sins which are detestable in the sight of God and all good people, as I have been saying.

Old Testament examples

In the first book of Moses, we read that when mankind began to be multiplied on the earth, the men and women gave their minds so greatly to fleshly delights and impure pleasure that they lived without all fear of God (Genesis 6-7). God, seeing this carnal and abominable living, and perceiving that they did not amend their lives but rather increased daily more and more in their sinful and unclean lifestyles, repented that he had ever made them. And to show how greatly he abhorred adultery, sexual immorality, fornication, and all uncleanness, he made all the foundations of the deep earth burst out, and the floodgates of heaven opened so that rain came down on the earth for forty days and forty nights. By this means, he destroyed the whole world and all mankind, all except eight people: Noah, the "preacher of righteousness" as St Peter calls him (2 Peter 2:5), his wife, his three sons, and their wives. What a grievous judgment God sent here on all living creatures, for the sin of sexual immorality. Because of this, God took vengeance not only on mankind but also on birds, beasts, and all living creatures. Murder had been committed before, but the world had not been destroyed for that. But for sexual immorality, the world (apart from a few) was overwhelmed with water and so perished. An example worthy to be remembered, so that you may learn to fear God.[3]

Again, we read that for the filthy sin of uncleanness, Sodom and Gomorrah and the other cities near to them were destroyed with fire and brimstone from heaven, so that there was neither man, woman, child, or beast there left alive, nor anything that grew on the earth (Genesis 19:1-29). Whose heart does not tremble at the hearing of this history? Who is so drowned in sexual immorality and uncleanness that they will not now and forever leave

---

3 It was not unusual for commentators to point to sexual immorality and fleshly lust as the sins in Genesis 6:1-5, which caused God's displeasure and the subsequent flood. See for example the comments of the Reformer Ulrich Zwingli (1484-1531) in John L. Thompson, Timothy George, and Scott M. Manetsch (eds.), *Genesis 1–11* (Reformation Commentary on Scripture; Downers Grove, IL: IVP Academic, 2012), 233–234, "Moses does not say merely that they had taken wives for themselves, ... but he magnifies the guilt of those who seized wives and daughters sheerly from lust. Indeed, he explains why such shameful deeds inundated the earth, so that even pious people clung to carnal affections. For this is the power of the flesh, this its character, that even the pious and 'the sons of God' are captivated by concupiscence. The sons of God were thus knocked off course: they were guided more by the affections of the flesh than by the fear of God; they gave more consideration to what concupiscence demanded than what rectitude requests."

this abominable lifestyle, seeing that God grievously punishes uncleanness, to rain fire and brimstone from heaven to destroy whole cities, to kill man, woman, and child, and all other living creatures who lived there, to consume with fire all that ever grew? What can be more manifest tokens of God's wrath and vengeance against uncleanness and impurity of life? Mark this history (good people), and fear the vengeance of God.

Do we not also read that God struck Pharaoh and his house with great plagues because of his ungodly desire for Sarai, the wife of Abraham (Genesis 12:14-17)? Likewise we read of Abimelech, King of Gerar, although he did not touch her or sleep with her (Genesis 20:1-7). God cast these plagues and punishments on impure and unclean people before the Law was given to declare how great his love for marriage is (the law of nature alone reigning in the hearts of humanity). The Law would later declare how much he abhors adultery, fornication, and all uncleanness. And when the Law that forbade sexual sin was given by Moses to the Jews, did not God command that those who broke it should be put to death? The words of the Law are these: "Whoever commits adultery with another man's wife shall be put to death—both the man and the woman—because they have broken the bond of marriage" (Leviticus 20:10). In the Law it was also commanded that a woman and a man caught together in sexual sin should both be stoned to death (Deuteronomy 22:23-24).

In another place we also read that God commanded Moses to take all the chiefs and leaders of the people, and to hang them on gallows openly so that everyone could see them, because they committed or did not punish sexual immorality (Numbers 25:4). And again, did not God send such a plague among the people, for fornication and uncleanness, that twenty-three thousand died in one day (Numbers 25:9; 1 Corinthians 10:8)?

I pass over for lack of time the many other histories in the holy Bible which declare the grievous vengeance and heavy displeasure of God against the sexually immoral and adulterers. Certainly, this extreme punishment appointed by God evidently shows how greatly God hates sexual immorality. So let us not doubt that God at this present time abhors all manner of uncleanness, no less than he did under the old Law, and will undoubtedly punish it, both in this world and in the world to come. For he is a God who can abide no wickedness. Therefore, all who care for the glory of God and the salvation of their souls ought to avoid it.

St Paul says, "All these things are written for our example," and to teach us the fear of God and obedience to his holy law (1 Corinthians 10:6, 11). For if God did not spare the natural branches, neither will he spare us who are only grafted on, if we commit such offences (Romans 11:21-22). If God destroyed many thousands of people, many cities, indeed the whole world, because of sexual immorality, let us not flatter ourselves and think that we shall escape and be free without punishment. For he has promised in his holy law to send most grievous plagues on those who disobey his holy commandments.

Civil punishments

Thus we have heard how God punishes the sin of adultery. Let us now hear about certain laws which the civil magistrates devised in various countries for the punishment of it. Then we will learn how uncleanness has always been detested in all well-ordered cities and commonwealths, and among all honest persons.

The law among the Lepreians was this: that when anyone was caught in adultery, they were bound and carried for three days through the city and afterwards, as long as they lived, they were despised and with shame considered as people without any honesty.[4] Among the Locrians, adulterers had both of their eyes thrust out.[5] The Romans in times past punished sexual immorality

---

4   Lepreum was an ancient Greek city-state, near the present village of Lepreo in southern Greece.

5   Locris was a region of ancient central Greece, home to the Locrensians or Locrians.

sometimes by fire, sometimes by sword. If a man among the Egyptians was taken in adultery, the law was that he should openly, in the presence of all the people, be whipped naked a thousand times; the woman that was caught with him had her nose cut off, and so was always identified as an adulteress and therefore to be abhorred by all. Among the Arabians, those who were caught in adultery had their heads cut off. The Athenians punished sexual immorality by death in a similar way. So likewise did the barbarous Tartars.[6] Among the Turks, even today, those caught in adultery, both man and woman, are stoned to death straightaway without mercy.[7]

Thus we see what godly laws were devised in times past by the authorities, for putting away sexual immorality and for maintaining holy marriage and pure relationships. And the author of these laws were not Christians, but unbelievers. Yet they were so inflamed with the love of honesty and purity of life, that for the maintenance and conservation of it they made godly statutes, allowing neither fornication nor adultery to reign in their realms unpunished. Christ said to the people: "The people of Nineveh will rise at the judgment with this nation (meaning the unfaithful Jews) and shall condemn them. For they repented at the preaching of Jonah, but behold," he said, "one greater than Jonah is here (meaning himself), and yet you do not repent" (Matthew 12:41). So do you not think that in the same way, the Locrians, Arabians, Athenians, and the others will rise up at the judgment and condemn us? They ceased their sexual immorality at human com-

---

6   Inhabitants of Tartary, the name given at this time to the area of Manchuria, Siberia, and Central Asia from which the Mongol Empire had sprung in the 13th century.

7   The information in this paragraphs comes almost verbatim from Heinrich Bullinger's book *The Christian State of Matrimony*, which was translated by Miles Coverdale and published in various editions in Antwerp and London between 1541 and 1552, and the preface to it by Thomas Becon (1511-1567), who was one of Cranmer's chaplains and the author of this homily. They drew on information in Andreas Tiraquellus, *De Legibus Connubialibus et Iure Maritali* (Paris, 1524), and Joannes Boemus, *Repertorium Librorum Trium... de Omnium Gentium Ritibus* (Paris, 1520).

mand, and we have the law and clear precepts and commandments of God—and yet we do not forsake our impure lifestyles. Truly, truly, it shall be easier on the day of judgment for those unbelieving people than for us, unless we repent and change.

Although physical death seems to us a grievous punishment in this world for sexual immorality, yet that pain is nothing in comparison to the grievous torments which adulterers, fornicators, and all unclean persons shall suffer after this life. For all such people shall be excluded and shut out of the kingdom of heaven, as St Paul says: "Do not be deceived: neither the sexually immoral, nor idolaters, nor adulterers, nor men who have sex with other men, nor thieves, nor the greedy, nor drunkards, nor slanderers, nor swindlers will inherit the kingdom of God" (1 Corinthians 6:9-10; Galatians 5:19-21; Ephesians 5:5). And St John in his Revelation says that the sexually immoral shall have their part with murderers, sorcerers, enchanters, liars, idolators and such others, in the lake which burns with fire and brimstone, which is the second death (Revelation 21:8). The punishment of the body, although it is death, has an end; but the punishment of the soul, which St John calls "the second death" is everlasting: there shall be fire and brimstone, weeping and gnashing of teeth, and the worm which there gnaws the conscience of the damned shall never die (Matthew 13:42; Mark 9:43-48; Luke 3:17; Isaiah 66:24).

O whose heart does not distil even drops of blood to hear and consider these things? If we tremble and shake at the hearing and naming of these pains, O what shall those who feel them do when they suffer them, and suffer them forever? God have mercy on us. Who is now so drowned in sin and past all godliness, that they will be more concerned for an impure pleasure (which soon passes away) than by the loss of everlasting glory? Again, who will so give themselves to the lusts of the flesh that they do not fear the pains of hell fire at all?

KEEP YOUR HEARTS PURE

But now let us hear how we may avoid the sin of sexual immorality, so we may walk in the fear of God and be free from those most grievous and intolerable torments which afflict all unclean persons. To avoid fornication, adultery, and all uncleanness, let us ensure that above all things, we keep our hearts pure and clean from all evil thoughts and carnal lusts. For if our heart is so infected and corrupted, we fall headlong into all kinds of ungodliness. This we shall easily do if, when we feel inwardly that Satan our old enemy tempts us to sexual immorality, we by no means consent to his crafty suggestions but valiantly resist and withstand him by strong faith in the word of God. We must always bring against him in our heart this commandment of God: *Scriptum est, non moechaberis*; "It is written, 'You shall not commit sexual sin'" (Matthew 5:27; Exodus 20:14).[8]

It would be good also for us to always live in the fear of God and to set before our eyes the grievous threatenings of God against all ungodly sinners. And we should consider in our minds how impure, carnal, and brief that pleasure is to which Satan moves us. And again, how the pain appointed as punishment for that sin is intolerable and everlasting. Moreover, we must be moderate and sober in eating and drinking, avoid unclean conversation, avoid all immoral company, flee idleness, delight in reading holy scripture, and watch in godly prayers and virtuous meditations. And at all times to endure godly trials shall help greatly in the avoidance of sexual sin.

Here are all sorts of people to be admonished, whether they are married or unmarried, to love chastity and cleanness of life. For the married are bound by the law of God, so purely to love one another that neither of them seek any other love. The man must only join to his wife, and the wife only to her husband. They

---

8   It is noteworthy that the Homily actually quotes the Latin here as well as the English, as if the word of God was being wielded like a spell against an enemy, although more like Christ (see Matthew 4:1-11) than Harry Potter.

must so delight in one another's company that neither of them covet any other. And as they are bound to live together like this in all godliness and honesty, so likewise is it their duty to bring up their children, that they do not fall into Satan's snare or into any uncleanness, but that they may come pure and honest to holy marriage in due time.

So likewise ought all masters and rulers to provide that no sexual immorality or any kind of uncleanness is indulged in by their servants. And again, those who are single and feel in themselves that they cannot live without the company of a spouse, let them marry and so live together in a godly way. For it is better to marry than to burn (1 Corinthians 7:9). And to avoid fornication, the apostle says "each man should have sexual relations with his own wife, and each woman with her own husband" (1 Corinthians 7:2). Finally, all such as feel in themselves a sufficiency and ability (through the operation of God's Spirit) to lead a single and self-controlled life, let them praise God for his gift, and seek by all means possible to maintain this, by reading holy scriptures, by godly meditations, by continual prayers, and other such virtuous exercises.

If we all endeavour to behave in this way—to avoid fornication, adultery, and all uncleanness, and lead our lives in all godliness and honesty, serving God with a pure and clean heart, and glorifying him in our bodies by leading an innocent life—we may be sure to be in the number of those of whom our saviour Christ speaks in the Gospel thus: "Blessed are the pure in heart, for they shall see God" (Matthew 5:8)—to whom alone be all glory, honour, rule, and power, forever and ever, *Amen.*

STRIFE AND
CONTENTION

Today (good Christian people), I shall declare to you the unprofitableness and shameful dishonesty of contention, strife, and argument. So, when you see (as it were, in a scene painted before your eyes) the defectiveness and deformity of this most detestable vice which so tends towards evil, your stomachs may be moved to rise against it, and to detest and abhor that sin which is so much to be hated, and so pernicious and hurtful to all.

UNITY NOT QUARRELS

Among all kinds of contention, none is more hurtful than contention in matters of religion. "Have nothing to do with foolish, ignorant controversies," says St Paul, "because you know that they breed quarrels. The servant of God must not be quarrelsome but kind to everyone" (2 Timothy 2:23-24; 1 Timothy 1:4). In St Paul's time, there was such contention and strife among the Corinthians; and at the moment we have the same among us English. For there are too many people, in alehouses or other places, who delight to argue about certain questions, not so as to build people up in the truth but for vain glory, and showing off their cunning. And so un-soberly do they reason and dispute that when neither party will

---

* The original title of this Homily was *An Homily against Contention and Brawling*.

give place to the other they fall to criticism and contention, and sometimes from hot words to further improper behaviour.

St Paul could not abide to hear among the Corinthians these words of discord or dissension, "'I follow Paul,' or 'I follow Apollos,' or 'I follow Cephas'" (1 Corinthians 1:12, 3:4). What would he then say if he heard these words of contention (which are now in almost everyone's mouth), "He is a Pharisee; she is an evangelical; he is of the new sort; she is of the old faith; he is a sound chap; he is a good catholic father; she is a liberal; she is a heretic." O how the church is divided! O how the cities are cut and mangled! O how the coat of Christ, that was seamless, is all pulled apart and torn (John 19:23)! O mystical body of Christ, where is that holy and happy unity, without which we are not in Christ? If one member is pulled from another, where is the body? If the body is taken from the head, where is the life of the body? We cannot be joined to Christ our head, unless we are glued together with concord and love, one to another (Ephesians 4:15-16). For the one who is not in this unity is not part of the church of Christ, which is a congregation or uniting together, not a dividing.

St Paul says that as long as there is jealousy, contention, and factions among us, we are worldly, and walk according to the flesh (1 Corinthians 3:4). And St James says, "if you harbour bitter envy and selfish ambition in your hearts, do not boast about it... For where you have envy and selfish ambition, there you find disorder and every evil practice" (James 3:14, 16). Why do we not hear St Paul who urges us (when he might command us), saying, "I appeal to you in the name of our Lord Jesus Christ, that all of you agree with one another in what you say and that there be no divisions among you, but that you be perfectly united in mind and thought" in the truth (1 Corinthians 1:10). If his desire is reasonable and honest, why do we not grant it? If his request is for our profit, why do we refuse it? And if we do not wish to hear his petition or prayer, let us then hear his urging, where he says:

"I urge you to live a life that is worthy of the calling you have received. Be completely humble and gentle. Be patient, and bear with one another in love. Make every effort to maintain the unity of the Spirit through the bond of peace. There is one body and one Spirit, just as you were called to one hope when you were called; one Lord, one faith, one baptism" (Ephesians 4:1-5).

There is, he says, only *one body*—and one cannot be a living member of it if one is at variance with the other members. There is *one Spirit*, who joins and knits all things together in one—and how can this one Spirit reign in us when we are divided among ourselves? There is only *one faith*—and how can we then say, "He is of the old faith, and she is of the new faith"? There is only *one baptism*—so are not all those who are baptised, one? Contention causes division, therefore it ought not to exist among Christians who are joined in a unity in one faith and one baptism. But if we show contempt for St Paul's request and exhortation, we must at least regard his earnest plea in which he very earnestly charges us and summons us in this way:

> "If you have any encouragement from being united with Christ, or any comfort from his love, or any participation in the Spirit, or any tenderness and compassion—then make my joy complete by being of the same mind, having the same love, being one in spirit and of one mind. Do not do anything out of selfish ambition or vain conceit" (Philippians 2:1-3).

Who, with any compassion, will not be moved by these pithy words? Whose heart is so stony that the sword of these words, which is sharper than any two-edged sword (Hebrews 4:12), may not cut and break them apart? Therefore, let us endeavour to make St Paul's joy in these verses complete, which shall eventually be for our great joy in another place.

HUMBLE BIBLE READING

Let us so read the scripture that by reading it we may be made better livers, rather than more contentious disputers. If anything is necessary to be taught, reasoned, or disputed, let us do it with all meekness, softness, and gentleness. If anything happens to be spoken disagreeably, let one bear another's frailty. Let those who are at fault rather amend than defend that which they have spoken amiss, in case they fall by contention from a foolish error into an obstinate heresy. For it is better, to give way meekly than to win the victory with a breach of love—which is what happens when everyone defends their opinion obstinately.

If we are Christians, why do we not follow Christ, who says, "Learn from me, for I am gentle and lowly of heart" (Matthew 11:29)? A disciple must learn the lesson of their schoolmaster, and a servant must obey the commandment of their master. "Who is wise and understanding among you?" asks St James, "By their good conduct let them show their works in the meekness of wisdom. But if you have bitter jealousy and selfish ambition in your hearts, do not boast and be false to the truth. This is not the wisdom that comes down from above, but is earthly, unspiritual, demonic" (James 3:13-17). But the wisdom that comes from above, from the Spirit of God, is simple and pure, corrupted with no evil affections; it is quiet, meek, and peaceable, abhorring all desire for contention; it is amenable, obedient, not grudging to learn and to give way to those who teach better for their reformation.

There shall never be an end of striving and contention if we contend about who shall be master and have the upper-hand in contention. We shall heap error upon error if we keep stubbornly defending that which was spoken rashly. For it is certainly true that stiffness in maintaining an opinion, breeds contention, brawling, and criticism which, along with other vices, is most damaging and destructive to common peace and quietness.

Don't feed the trolls
Quarrels are often between two people (for no one commonly criticises themselves), and involve two most detestable vices: one is picking quarrels, with sharp and contentious words; the other is giving argumentative replies and multiplying evil words in return.

The first is so abominable that St Paul says, "If anyone claims to be a brother or sister but is a worshipper of idols, a brawler, a picker of quarrels, a thief, or an extortioner, do not eat with such a person" (1 Corinthians 5:11). Consider here that St Paul numbers a scolder, a brawler, a picker of quarrels among thieves and idolators. Less hurt often comes from a thief than from a railing tongue. For one takes away a person's good name; the other takes away their wealth, which is of much less value and estimation than their good name. A thief only hurts the one they steal from; but the one who has an evil tongue troubles the whole town where they live, and sometimes the whole country. A ranting tongue is a pestilence so full of contagion, that St Paul wishes Christians to avoid the company of such people, and neither to eat nor drink with them. He does not wish a Christian woman to forsake her husband, even if he is an unbeliever (1 Corinthians 7:13), nor should a Christian servant leave their unbelieving master (1 Timothy 6:1-2). He allows Christians to keep company with unbelievers. Yet he forbids us to eat or drink with a scolder, a quarrel picker.

In 1 Corinthians 6 he says this: "Do not be deceived: Neither the sexually immoral nor idolaters nor thieves nor drunkards *nor slanderers* will dwell in the kingdom of heaven" (1 Corinthians 6:9-10). It must be a great fault which moves and causes a father to disinherit his natural son. And how can it be otherwise, but that cursed speaking, slander, must be a most damnable sin, which causes God, our most merciful and loving Father, to deprive us of his most blessed kingdom of heaven.

Against the other sin, that is returning taunt for taunt, Christ himself speaks: "I say to you," says our saviour Christ, "do not resist evil, but love your enemies and speak well of those who speak evil of you. Do good to those who do evil to you, and pray for those who hurt and pursue you, that you may be children of your Father who is in heaven, who causes his sun to rise on both the evil and the good, and sends his rain to both the just and the unjust" (Matthew 5:39, 44-45). The teaching of St Paul agrees very well with this doctrine of Christ: that chosen vessel of God (Acts 9:15) never ceases to exhort us and call on us to, "Bless those who curse you. Bless, I say, and do not curse. Do not repay anyone evil for evil. If it is possible, as far as it depends on you, live peaceably with all" (Romans 12:14, 17-18).

How to Take Insults

It has been declared to you in this sermon against strife and brawling what great misfortune comes from it, and especially from contention in matters of religion. It has been declared how, when no one will give way to another, there is no end of contention and discord, and that unity which God requires of Christians is utterly neglected and broken. And I have said that this contention consists chiefly in two things: picking quarrels, and making argumentative answers.

Impatience

Now you shall hear St Paul's words: "Dearly beloved, do not avenge yourselves, but rather leave room for God's wrath, for it is written 'Vengeance is mine, I will revenge,' says the Lord. Therefore, if your enemy is hungry, feed them; if they are thirsty, give them drink. Do not be overcome with evil, but overcome evil with goodness" (Romans 12:19-21; Deuteronomy 32:35). All these are the words of St Paul. But those who are so puffed up and think so much of themselves that they cannot abide so much as one critical word to be spoken about them will perhaps say, "If I am reviled, shall I stand by like a goose or a fool, with my hand over my mouth? Shall I be such an idiot and simpleton to suffer everyone to speak about me whatever they like, to rant as they like, to spew out all their venom against me as they please? Is it not more fitting that the one who speaks such evil should be answered accordingly? If I use such gentleness and softness, I shall both increase my enemy's argumentativeness, and provoke others to do the same." Such are the reasons people give in defence of their impatience.

Is there a hope of remedying argumentativeness, by answering argumentative people with argumentativeness? If so, it would be less offensive to answer in that way, not from anger or malice but only in order to reform the one who is so argumentative or malicious. But if one cannot amend someone else's fault, or cannot amend it without a fault of your own, it is better that one should perish than two. If you cannot quiet them with gentle words, at least do not follow them in wicked and uncharitable words. If you can pacify them with suffering, then suffer; and if not, it is better to suffer evil than to do evil, to speak well than to speak evil. For to speak well against evil comes from the Spirit of God, but to render evil for evil comes from the opposite spirit.

The one who cannot temper or rule their own anger is weak and feeble, and not a strong person. For true strength is to overcome wrath and to think little of injury and other people's foolishness. Besides, when one thinks little of the wrong done to them by their enemy, everyone perceives that it was spoken or done without cause; whereas, on the contrary, the one who fumes and is inflamed at such things helps the cause of their adversary by creating suspicion that the thing they allege is actually true. And so in trying to avenge evil, we show ourselves to be evil; and while we want to punish another person's folly, we double and enhance our own folly.

Forgiveness

Those who wish to excuse their own impatience find many pretences to do so. "My enemy," they say, "is not worthy to have gentle words or deeds, being so full of malice and argumentativeness." The less they are worthy, the more you are encouraged by God, the more you are commended by Christ (for whose sake you should render good for evil), because he has commanded you and also deserves your obedience in this. Your neighbour has perhaps offended you with a word: remember with how many words and deeds, how grievously you have offended your Lord God. What was mankind when Christ died for us? Were we not his enemy, and unworthy to have his favour and mercy? Even so, with what gentleness and patience does he forbear and tolerate and suffer you, although he is daily offended by you?

Forgive your neighbour a light trespass, therefore, that Christ may forgive you (who every day are an offender) many thousands of trespasses. For if you forgive your brother or sister, when they sin against you, then you have a sure sign and token that God (to whom all are debtors or trespassers) will forgive you. How would you have God be merciful to you, if you are cruel to your brother or sister? Can you not find it in your heart to do that towards another (who is your fellow), which God has done to you (who are but his servant)? Ought not one sinner to forgive another, seeing that Christ who was no sinner, prayed to his Father for those who spitefully and without mercy put him to death? "When he was reviled, he did not revile in return, and when he suffered wrongfully, he did not threaten but entrusted himself to the one who judges justly" (1 Peter 2:23).

What do you think of your Head? If you do not labour to be in the body, you cannot be a member of Christ—if you do not follow in the steps of Christ who (as the prophet says) was "led like a lamb to the slaughter" (Isaiah 53:7), not opening his mouth to revile, but opening his mouth to pray for those who crucified him, saying "Father, forgive them, for they do not know what they are doing" (Luke 23:34). Immediately after Christ, St Stephen followed this example (Acts 7:60), and after him, St Paul: "When we are insulted, we bless. When we are persecuted, we bear it. When we are slandered, we answer kindly" (1 Corinthians 4:12-13). As St Paul taught, so he did; and what he did, he taught. "Bless", he said, "those who persecute you. Bless and do not curse" (Romans 12:14). Is it a great thing to speak well of your adversary, to whom Christ commands you to do good? David, when Shimei cursed him, did not scold him in return, but said patiently, "Let him curse. Perhaps the Lord will have mercy on me" (2 Samuel 16:11-12).

COPING WITH INSULTS

Histories are full of examples of unbelievers who took very meekly both abusive words and harmful deeds. And shall those unbelievers excel in patience more than us who profess Christ, the teacher and example of patience? Lysander, when someone was raging against him, reviling him, was not moved but said, "Go on, go on, speak against me as much and as often you want, and leave nothing out, if it means you may be able to empty yourself of the vicious notions with which you seem to be fully laden."[1] Many people speak evil of everyone, because they can speak well of no one. This wise man avoided people of this sort and their injurious words spoken against him, imputing and putting them down to the natural sickness of his adversary.

Pericles, when a certain scolder or ranting fellow reviled him, answered him back not a word, but went home. As night fell, this scolder followed him raging still more and more because he saw that Pericles was taking no notice. When he arrived home it was dark, so Pericles commanded one of his servants to light a torch and take the ranter home safely to his own house.[2] He not only suffered this brawler quietly and patiently, but also repaid an evil deed with a good one, and that to his enemy.

Is it not a shame for us, who profess Christ, to be worse than unbelieving people, in a thing of chief importance to Christ's religion? Shall philosophy persuade them, more than God's word shall persuade us? Shall natural reason prevail more with them, than religion does with us? Shall human wisdom lead them to that, to which heavenly doctrine cannot lead us? What blindness, wilfulness, or rather madness is this? Pericles was provoked to anger by many insulting words, but answered not a word. But we, stirred by one little word—what tragedies do we claim! How do we fume,

---

1   See Plutarch's, *Moralia* III (LCL 245:376-377), Lysander, 13 (229 E). Lysander (died 395 BC) was a Spartan general.

2   See Plutarch, *Lives* (LCL 065:12-13), Pericles, 5.1 (154 C). Pericles (495-429 BC) was an Athenian general and statesman.

rage, stamp and stare like mad men! Many people make a great matter out of every trifle, and with the spark of a little word will kindle a great fire, taking everything in the worst possible way. But how much better is it, and more like the example and doctrine of Christ, to make a great fault in our neighbour into a small thing, reasoning with ourselves in this way: "They spoke these words, but it was in a sudden heat, or the drink spoke them, but it was not them"; or, "They were prompted by someone else to speak them, or they said this because they were ignorant of the truth"; or "They spoke them, not against me but against the person they thought me to be."

THINK OF THE FUTURE

When it comes to speaking evil against other people: first, let us examine ourselves, whether we are faultless and clear of the fault which we find in others. For it is a shame when someone who blames another for a fault is guilty themselves either of the same fault or an even greater one. It is a shame for the one who is blind to call another person blind; and it is more shameful for the one who is completely blind to call someone else blinkered, who is only partially blind. For this is to see a speck of sawdust in someone else's eye when you have a plank in your own eye (Matthew 7:3-5). So let us consider, that the one who speaks badly of other people shall commonly also be spoken of badly. And the one who takes pleasure in speaking how they like, shall be compelled to hear what they do not like, to their displeasure. Moreover, let them remember the saying that we "shall give an account for every idle word" (Matthew 12:36). How much more then shall we have to give an account for our sharp, bitter, brawling, and critical words, which provoke our brothers and sisters to be angry. We shall have to give an account for this breach of love.

When it comes to evil replies: even if we are extremely provoked by other people's evil speaking, yet we should not follow their argumentativeness by answering evil with evil. We must consider that anger is a kind of madness, and that the one who is angry is (as it were, for a time) in a frenzy. Therefore, let us beware, lest in fury we say something which we may afterwards rightly regret. And the one who would defend themselves and say, "Anger is not the same as fury", and that they have their reason even when they are most angry, let them reason like this with themselves when they are angry: "Now I am so moved and inflamed but in a little while I may have changed my mind. So then, why should I say something now in my anger which cannot be changed later if I do change my mind? Why should I do anything now being (as it were) out of my mind, about which I shall be very sad when I come to myself again? Why do I not do *now*, the thing which I know time will eventually persuade me of? Surely reason, godliness, and indeed Christ, demand that?"

If someone is called an adulterer, usurer, drunkard, or any other insulting name, let them earnestly consider whether they are called this truly or falsely. If truly, let them amend their fault, so that their adversary may not afterwards rightly charge them with such offences. If these things are laid against them falsely, let them consider whether they have given any occasion to be suspected of such things. And so they may both cut off that suspicion which gave rise to the slander, and in other things they shall live more warily. And behaving in this way, we may take no hurt, but rather much good, from the rebukes and slanders of our enemy. For the reproach of an enemy may be to many people a more effective spur to the amendment of their life than the gentle warning of a friend. Philip the King of Macedon, when he was badly spoken of by the chief rulers of the city of Athens, thanked them heartily, because he was made better by them, both in his words and deeds. "For I endeavour," he said, "both by my sayings and doings to prove them liars."[3]

---

3 Plutarch, *Moralia* III (LCL 245:42-43), Philip the Father of Alexander, 7 (177 E). Philip II (382-336 BC) was King of Macedon in Greece, and father of Alexander the Great.

3. Answering an Adversary

You heard in the last part of this sermon against strife and brawling how we may answer those who maintain their argumentativeness in contentions, and those who want to avenge with words such evils as other people do to them. And finally, you heard how we may, according to God's will, order ourselves, and what we should think about others when we are provoked to contention and strife with railing words. Now, to proceed on this subject, you need to know the right way to counter and overcome our adversary and enemy.

Answering a fool

This is the best way to counter an adversary: so to live, that all those who know your honesty may bear witness that you are slandered unworthily. If the fault for which you are slandered is such that for the defence of your honesty you need to make an answer, answer quietly and softly in this fashion, that those faults are laid against you falsely. For it is true what the wise man says: "A soft answer turns away anger, and a hard and sharp answer stirs up rage and fury"(Proverbs 15:1). The sharp answer of Nabal provoked David to cruel vengeance; but the gentle words of Abigail quenched the fire that was all in a flame (1 Samuel 25:9-35). And a special remedy against malicious tongues is to arm ourselves with patience, meekness, and silence; lest with multiplying words with the enemy, we are made as evil as them.

But those who cannot bear one evil word, perhaps, for their own excuse will cite what is written: "The one who despises his good name is cruel."[4] Also we read, "Answer a fool according to their foolishness" (Proverbs 26:5). And our Lord Jesus held his peace at certain evil sayings, but to others he answered diligently.

4   Augustine's Sermon 355, *De Vita et Moribus Clericorum Suorum* 1.1 (PL 39:1569) also cited in Gratian's *Decretum, Pars Secunda*, C 12 q.1 c.10 (PL 187:886). John Rotelle (ed.), *Sermons III/10 (341- 400) on Various Subjects* (translated by Edmund Hill; Hyde Park, NY: New City Press, 1995).

He heard people call him a Samaritan, a carpenter's son, a wine drinker, and he held his peace (John 19:9; Matthew 11:19, 13:55); but when he heard them say, "You have a devil within you" (John 8:48), he answered to that earnestly.

It is indeed true that there is a time when it is appropriate to "answer a fool according to their foolishness, in case they should seem in their own conceit to be wise" (Proverbs 26:5). And sometimes, it is not profitable to "answer a fool according to their foolishness", in case the wise person is made to look like the fool (Proverbs 26:4). When our infamy (or the reproach that is done to us) is joined with the peril of many, then it is necessary in answering to be quick and ready. For we read that many holy people of good zeal have sharply and fiercely spoken and answered tyrants and evil people. These sharp words came not from anger, rancour, or malice, or desire for vengeance, but from a fervent desire to bring them to the true knowledge of God, and from ungodly living, by an earnest and sharp rebuke and reprimand.

Answering with zeal

In this zeal, St John the Baptist called the Pharisees "brood of vipers" (Matthew 3:7); and St Paul called the Galatians "fools" (Galatians 3:1); and the people of Crete he called "liars, evil beasts, lazy gluttons" (Titus 1:12); and the false apostles he called "dogs and crafty workmen" (Philippians 3:2). And this zeal is godly and to be allowed, as it is plainly proven by the example of Christ who, although he was the fountain and spring of all meekness, gentleness, and softness, yet he called the obstinate Scribes and Pharisees "blind guides, fools, whitewashed tombs, hypocrites, serpents, a brood of vipers, a corrupt and wicked generation" (Matthew 23:16-33, 12:39). Also, he rebuked Peter eagerly, saying, "Get behind me, Satan" (Matthew 16:23). Likewise, St Paul rebuked Elymas, saying, "You are a son of the Devil, an enemy of everything that is right! You are full of every kind of deceit and trickery. Will you never stop perverting the straight paths of the Lord? Now, behold, the hand of the Lord is against you. You will be blind, and not even able to see the light of the sun for a time" (Acts 13:10-11). Also, St Peter rebuked Ananias very sharply saying, "Ananias, how is it that Satan has filled your heart so much that you should lie to the Holy Spirit?" (Acts 5:3).

This zeal has been so fervent in many good people, that it has stirred them not only to speak bitter and eager words, but also to do things which might seem to some to be cruel. But indeed, they are very just, loving, and godly, because they were not done out of anger, malice, or a contentious mind, but from a fervent desire for the glory of God and the correction of sin, executed by people called to that office. For in this zeal, our Lord Jesus Christ drove the buyers and sellers out of the Temple with a whip (John 2:15). In this zeal, Moses broke the two tablets which he had received from God's hand, when he saw the Israelites dancing around a calf, and caused three thousand of his own people to be killed (Exodus 32:15-19, 27-28). In this zeal, Phineas the son of Eleazar thrust his sword through Zimri and Cozbi, whom he found together joined in the act of sexual immorality (Numbers 25:7-8, 14-15). These examples are not to be followed by everyone, however, but only as they called to office and set in authority.

AVOIDING STRIFE
Returning again to contentious words, and especially in matters of religion and God's word, which should be used with all modesty, sobriety, and love, the words of St James ought to be well noted and remembered, where he says that from contention rises all evil (James 3:16). And the wise King Solomon says, "It is to one's honour to avoid strife, but every fool is quick to quarrel" (Proverbs 20:3). And because this vice is so hurtful to the society of a commonwealth, in all well-ordered cities these common brawlers and critics are punished with a notable kind of pain, such as being being set on a cucking stool, pillory, or such like.[5] And those who

---

5   A *cucking stool* was a chair to which disorderly people were tied and then ducked

do as much as they can to brawl and criticise to disturb the quietness and peace of the realm are unworthy to live in it. And from where does this contention, strife, and disagreeableness come, but from pride and vainglory? Let us therefore "humble ourselves under the mighty hand of God" (1 Peter 5:6), who has promised to rest upon those who are humble and lowly in spirit (Luke 1:52; Isaiah 57:15).

If we are good and peaceable Christians, let it appear so in our speech and tongues. If we have forsaken the devil, let us no more use devilish tongues. The one who has been a railing critic, now let them be a sober counsellor. The one who has been a malicious slanderer, now let them be a loving comforter. The one who has been a vain ranter, now let them be a spiritual teacher. The one who has abused their tongue in cursing, now let them use it in blessing. The one who has abused their tongue in evil speaking, now let them use it in speaking well. "Let all bitterness, anger, malice, and slander be put away from you" (Ephesians 4:31).

If you can, and it is possible, in no way be angry. But if you cannot be completely clear of this passion, then so temper and bridle it, that it does not stir you up to contention and brawling. If you are provoked with evil speaking, arm yourself with patience, gentleness, and silence, either speaking nothing or else being very soft, meek, and gentle in answering. Overcome your adversaries with goodness and gentleness. And above all things, keep peace and unity. Do not be peace-breakers, but peace-makers. And then there is no doubt that God, the author of comfort and peace, will grant us peace of conscience, and such concord and agreement, "that with one mouth and mind we may glorify God, the Father of our Lord Jesus Christ" (Romans 15:6). To whom be all glory, now and forever, *Amen.*

---

into water or otherwise ridiculed, as a public punishment. A *pillory* was a wooden frame with holes for head and hands into which offenders were locked and exposed to public humiliation.

GLOSSARY

Ambrose *(339-397)* was Bishop of Milan in Italy.

Anselm *(1033-1109)* was Archbishop of Canterbury.

Augustine *(354-430)* was Bishop of Hippo in what is now Algeria.

Basil *(328-378)* was Bishop of Caesarea Mazaca in Cappadocia, in what is now Turkey.

Thomas Becon *(1511-1567)* was one of Thomas Cranmer's chaplains and the original author of *An Homily of Whoredom and Uncleanness.*

Bernard *(1090-1153)* was Abbot of Clairvaux in Burgundy, France.

Edmund Bonner *(1500-1569)* was Bishop of London, and the original author of *A Homily of Christian Love and Charity.*

Martin Bucer *(1491-1551)* was a German Reformer who ministered in Strasbourg and later as Regius Professor of Divinity at Cambridge.

Heinrich Bullinger *(1504-1575)* succeeded Zwingli as Pastor of the Grossmünster in Zürich, Switzerland.

John Calvin *(1509-1564)* was a pastor and theologian in Geneva, and originally from Noyon, France.

Chromatius *(died 406/407)* was Bishop of Aquileia, Italy.

John Chrysostom *(347-407)* was Bishop of Constantinople in what is now Turkey.

Miles Coverdale *(1488-1569)* was a Bible translator and Bishop of Exeter.

Thomas Cranmer *(1489-1556)* was Archbishop of Canterbury and the man behind much of the *Book of Common Prayer* and several of the *Homilies.*

Cyprian *(c.200-258)* was Bishop of Carthage in what is now Tunisia.

Didymus of Alexandria *(313-398)* or Didymus the Blind, was a theologian from Alexandria, Egypt.

John William Fletcher *(1729-1785)* from Nyon, Switzerland was a leading Wesleyan methodist minister in Madeley, Shropshire, England.

Fulgentius *(462-533)* was Bishop of Ruspe in what is now Tunisia.

Gregory the Great *(539-604)*, was Bishop of Rome.

William Grimshaw *(1708-1763)* was Vicar of Haworth in Yorkshire, England and a leading Evangelical preacher.

Edmund Grindal *(1519-1583)* was Archbishop of Canterbury.

John Harpsfield *(1516–1578)* was a Fellow of New College, Oxford, the first Regius Professor of Greek at Oxford, and the original author of *A Homily of the Misery of All Mankind and of their Condemnation to Death Everlasting, by Their Own Sin.*

Hervé of Déols *(c.1080-1150)* was a Benedictine Bible interpreter from the Abbey of Notre-Dame-du-Bourg-Dieu in Déols, Centre-Val de Loire, France.

Hilary *(314-366)* was Bishop of Poitiers in France.

Philip Edgcumbe Hughes *(1915-1990)* was the Secretary of Church Society and Editor of *Churchman.*

Jerome *(342-420)* was a Christian scholar from Stridon in what is now Croatia.

Peter Lombard *(1099-1159)* was Bishop of Paris in France.

Lysander *(died 395 BC)* was a Spartan general.

St Martin *(316-397)* was Bishop of Tours in France but was born in what is now Hungary.

Pelagius *(c.360-420)* was a British monk and teacher of the Roman aristocracy, who wrote commentaries on all of Paul's epistles, but whose teachings on original sin and predestination were condemned as heretical in 418.

Pericles *(495-429 BC)* was an Athenian general and statesman.

Oecumenius was from Greece or what is now Turkey, and wrote Bible commentaries sometime between the 6th-10th centuries.

Origen (185-254) was a biblical scholar from Alexandria, Egypt.

Philip II *(382-336 BC)* was King of Macedon in Greece, and father of Alexander the Great.

Photius *(c. 820–c. 891)* was Patriarch of Constantinople in what is now Turkey.

Prosper *(c.390-c.455)* was a lay theologian from Aquitaine in France.

Edward Seymour *(1506-1552)* was the Earl of Hertford and Duke of Somerset, brother of Henry VIII's third wife, Jane, and Lord Protector in the reign of his nephew, Edward VI.

Sulpicius Severus *(363-425)* was a Christian writer from Aquitaine in France.

Charles Simeon *(1759-1836)* was the Vicar of Holy Trinity, Cambridge.

Theophylact *(c.1050-1107)* was a Bible commentator and Archbishop of Ohrid in what is now North Macedonia.

Augustus Montague Toplady *(1740-1778)* from Farnham in Surrey, England was a leading Anglican Evangelical minister, historian, and hymn writer.

Peter Martyr Vermigli *(1499-1562)* was from Florence, Italy and served as Regius Professor of Divinity at Oxford under Edward VI.

George Whitefield *(1714-1778)* was an Anglican Evangelical preacher during the Great Awakening in Britain and America.

Ulrich Zwingli *(1484-1531)* was Pastor of the Grossmünster in Zürich, Switzerland.

INDEX OF PERSONS

SCRIPTURE INDEX

The Church of England's Official Sermons

Job
9:28 — 46
14:1-4 — 44-45
42:6 — 44

Psalm
1:2 — 42
5:5-6 — 65
19:7 — 35
19:10 — 35
19:12 — 47
27:9 — 124
32 — 59
32:1 — 82
40:12 — 47
51 — 46
51:1-10 — 50
51:5 — 47
51:11 — 124
56:11 — 158
63:11 — 108
66 — 132
78:30-31 — 123
84:3 — 83,84
89 — 59
90:17 — 83
95:11 — 121
103:3 — 51
106:6 — 49
116 — 141
116:7 — 141
116:15 — 140
118:6 — 158
119:103 — 35
119:105 — 35
119:130 — 35
130:7 — 50
143:2 — 46,50
143:7 — 124
150:6 — 110

Proverbs
2:14 — 166
8:15-17 — 147
8:17 — 147
15:1 — 188
20:3 — 190
24:16 — 46
26:4 — 189
26:5 — 188
26:5 — 189

Ecclesiastes
7:20 — 46
10:20 — 154-155

Song of Songs
6:10 — 28

Isaiah
5:1-6 — 122
5:1-7 — 121
5:13 — 37
5:24 — 37
11:2 — 126
29:13 — 89
31:1,3 — 118
38:20 — 165
40:6-7 — 44
42:8 — 110
47:9 — 88
47:13 — 88
53:7 — 102,184
57:15 — 191
63:16 — 74
66:24 — 174

Jeremiah
4:2 — 107,109
6:26 — 44
7:24 — 118
17:7-8 — 71
19:13 — 88
22:29 — 45
25:34 — 44
27:9 — 87

Ezekiel
18:23 — 126
18:32 — 126
33:11 — 126
33:12 — 126
33:14-16 — 126
33:19 — 126

Daniel
3:13-28 — 73
6:16-23 — 73
9:5 — 49
9:7 — 49

Hosea
4:12 — 117
5:4-6 — 117
5:5 — 117
9:10 — 88
13:9 — 52
14:2 — 127

Amos
5:26 — 87

Habakkuk
2:4 — 71

Zephaniah
1:5 — 87

Zechariah
5:1-4 — 115
7:9-14 — 118

Malachi
3:1 — 46
3:5 — 115

Matthew
1:21 — 51
3:7 — 189
3:11-14 — 46
4:1-11 — 175
4:4 — 34,35
5:8 — 176
5:27 — 175
5:27-28 — 160
5:33-37 — 111
5:34-37 — 111
5:39 — 181
5:43-47 — 100
5:44-45 — 181
6:19 — 141
6:23 — 82
7:3-5 — 186
7:8 — 40
7:15-20 — 93
7:24 — 36
9:12 — 47
10:37 — 100
10:42 — 142
11:9-11 — 46
11:19 — 189
11:29 — 180
12:1-14 — 90